WESTBOUND

Dear Emma,

Enjoy the journey & let's have a lot of fun together!

Li

Oct 13, 2019

WESTBOUND

A Memoir: My Journey from Beijing to New York City

Li Tian, Ph.D.

Copyright © 2019 by Li Tian, Ph.D.

All rights reserved. No part of this publication may be reproduced, distributed, or transmitted in any form or by any means, including photocopying, recording, or any other electronic or mechanical methods, without the prior written permission of the publisher, except in the case of brief quotations embodied in critical reviews and certain other noncommercial uses permitted by copyright law.
For permission requests, email your request to:
Westbound.Book@gmail.com.

I have tried to recreate events, locales, and conversations from my memories of them. In order to maintain their anonymity, I have changed the names of most individuals, time and places in some instances. I may have changed some other characteristics and details such as physical properties, date and time, occupations and other details.

ISBN 978-1-0919-8722-7
Imprint independently published

Cover Image ©Carmentianya from Stock Free Images
Portrait by Maria Ding @minzhending

First Edition

To all who have helped and supported me

To my Mom, Dad, Gege, and my husband
for giving me a loving home,
and challenging me to continuously grow

And to the best gifts of my life,
Sean and Jayne.
You are my reasons,
and my excuses, for this book.

Risk
More than others think is safe.

Care
More than others think is wise.

Dream
More than others think is practical.

Expect
More than others think is possible.

~ *Claude T. Bissell*

CONTENTS

PROLOGUE
xi

BEIJING
1

WESTBOUND
47

NEW YORK CITY
101

ACKNOWLEDGMENTS
179

Prologue

In our lives, there are always those who leave a special mark, even if we may not notice or realize it at the time. Someone like Steve.

Dr. Steve Kazianis, 1966 - 2008, from New York University.

Steve passed away over ten years ago. (RIP, Steve.)

I learned from Francesco only a few weeks ago.

For many years, and for many reasons, I did not staying in touch with many friends. But the day after I finished the initial draft of this manuscript, I reached out to those who were mentioned here. Those who I still have some form of contact information for, even if that info was really old.

I told them that I had written my first book, a memoir. That they were in it. And if they would like, I'd be happy to share with them the relevant parts (or the entire manuscript), so they could review and provide their feedback.

That was when I heard from Francesco about Steve's passing. (You won't see their names until the New York City chapters.)

I was shocked. How could Steve - someone who was always laughing, often mischievous, and perpetually devoted to his research - be gone already? At such a young age?

I told Quinn the sad news. I was surprised that she did not already know. She was heartbroken by the tragedy. Quinn also reminded me of another loss that she had told me long ago, Yanli. Yanli was killed in a terrible accident right there in Washington Square, many years ago. I think

Yanli could be the Daisy in Chapter 15 of this book. Though I can no longer be so sure.

There were several others that I still haven't been able to get in touch with, whom I held fond memories of. I am always grateful for their help and friendship during that special period of time when I needed it the most. I hope to hear from them. And maybe, just maybe, if they somehow find and read this book, I hope they would reach out to me and reconnect. But most importantly, I hope that they are well. And if they remember me from back then, I hope that memory is as keen as mine for them.

Life is too short, and lonely, to live in isolation.

I know it, because I lived it.

As you can see in this book. There was a time that I lived such a solitary life, in the crowded streets of New York City, utterly alone. It was quite awful, still agonizing to look back even now, decades later.

Fortunately, I did not have to endure that for too long. As I found some old friends and some new ones. They helped me, to not be alone, to belong. And eventually, to become the person I am today.

I am publishing this book not because I think my journey was all that special, or unique. On the contrary, I believe that everyone has a special journey. And I would love to see more of us share more of ourselves with others.

Life is precious. Life is short.

Our families, friends, communities, and everyone else on this blue earth, make our lives so beautiful, and our time here, so treasurable, and so worth it.

So I hope you will like this book.

I hope you will enjoy this journey with me.

I hope you have wonderful companions in your own life.

That you enjoy every bit of life's up and downs.

And I would always love to hear from you.

This book is dedicated to you.

Beijing

*Life is either a daring adventure,
or nothing.*

~ Helen Keller

CHAPTER ONE

June 1990

IN THE LIGHT FOG OF THE EARLY MORNING GRAY, OUR TRAIN pulled into the next station.

Realizing there wasn't any chance for more sleep, I resigned from my mindless attempt to smooth over the little rough dent on the low ceiling of the train with my fingertips, and climbed down from the top berth.

Mom was already up. Sitting on her bottom bed, she was staring out of the window. "She is having trouble sleeping as well." I thought and sat down next to her. I bent up my knees and hugged them close. It was a rare treat to travel with Mom. Unlike all my previous travels sitting on the hard plastic bench for the entire time, we upgraded to the sleeping car for this trip back to my college. That had certainly made it so much more comfortable. So, why couldn't I enjoy this twenty-four-hour journey more and not be so stressed out and tense about it?

I took a deep breath and released my knees. Stretched my left hand behind Mom's back, I searched for that small canvas school bag of mine. It was hidden under Mom's pillow, tucked next to the dividing wall between our bunk beds and those on the other side. I gave a sigh of relief when I felt the rigid rectangular form of the tin lunch box inside. Grasping it across the top with my fingertips, I lifted it up slightly. "Oh good." I thought, "It still feels right with its weight."

It was not even six o'clock yet. And it was very quiet in our car. I looked around. All the other passengers in this compartment were still asleep. The snores from the big beefy guy across from us seemed louder now that the train had stopped. The two brothers who took the middle berths slept like mirror images of each other. And the young mother and her baby girl on the other top berth were cuddled cozily together. They were all slumbered in their dreamland still.

My eyes fell on another lunch box that we brought with us. Identical to the hidden one, though this one was sitting on top of the tiny yellow table propped up under the windowsill. Leaving my bag where it was, I picked up the lunch box on the table. The grey metal felt cold to the touch. Worn after years of use, it was rubbed shiny on its slightly rounded corners. I took off the rubber bands that Mom had placed across the box to hold the lid closed, and opened it. There were two cold and hard steamed buns and three cooked tea-eggs remained inside. Taking one of the brown eggs out, I replaced the lid, and peeled off the already cracked shell. The egg was cold and dry. I ate it slowly, tried to warm it up in my mouth before swallowing each bite, and then washed it down with the water from our equally worn and cold green canteen.

Still six more hours to go. I wondered if this would be my very last trip back to my University, 中国科学技术大学 (University of Science and Technology of China, aka USTC). It was one of the top schools in the country. On that campus, I had spent several years of my childhood, and most of the last five years as a college student. Would I ever be back again? To this place where I grew up, left, and returned? Where so many memories were held for me? I had no answer to that.

But at this moment, I didn't really care either. My focus was on the mission of this trip; the content in that lunch box inside my bag under Mom's pillow; the reason why Mom had come along with me on this journey; and why we had spent extra money to buy tickets for the sleeping car on this train.

The train resumed moving. Its rhythmic chugging felt familiar and comforting. The view outside was glorious. Even with the light fog, I could see far out across the flat plains, growing tall with rice crops. In the awaking light of the dawn, I saw large parts of the paddy field had already turned golden in color, forecasting a bountiful harvest. And yet, my thoughts could hardly stay on the scenery. It kept veering back to what was inside that lunch box under the pillow. Even though it was quite light, it weighed heavy in my stomach.

I changed seats with Mom as she went back to reading her book. So I could better enjoy the view outside, catch that morning breeze, and try to pull my thoughts away from that hidden box.

I relaxed my sight to the farmland further away, to avoid being sickened by the greenery zooming by along the railway track. The morning fog was retreating and the day would probably turn out hot and sticky like it often was in this part of the country.

My thoughts drifted back in time...

Ever since I started in the boarding program of my middle school when I was eleven years old, I had spent very little time at home. This past few months doing research work for my thesis in Beijing was such a special treat. It was the first and only time that I lived at home with my parents and 哥哥 (*Gege*, older brother) for a good stretch of time in the past decade.

Mom always said that I grew up "wild." Since I didn't get as much teaching and lecturing from the two prestigious, professional educators that I had for parents. I actually felt that I grew up just fine. Maybe a little too independent and headstrong. But I had been content. Life had been fair and enjoyable to me, always surrounded by friends and family.

Sure we never had many material possessions. But in the culture where I grew up, where 精神食粮 (Spiritual Food, aka Knowledge) was taught to be more important than actual food. And that 万般皆下品，唯有读书高 (No profession was as esteemed as the scholars.) meant that I was fortunate to be born into such a "high-class" family. Both my parents were graduates from top universities in China. And they both taught engineering as professors at USTC soon after it was founded, when the school was still located in the capital city.

In the midst of the Cultural Revolution, like many other families, my family moved to a remote city called Hefei when the University was uprooted and relocated there itself. I was only 3 years old then. Years later, as I was finishing elementary school, my parents left their jobs at USTC, and we moved back to Beijing due to Mom's health issues.

I was grateful for having such smart and loving parents, and the life experience for living in different cities and environments, regardless of what things we got to have, and what food we had to eat. In fact, because of my talented and creative parents, *Gege* and I never truly starved. No matter how undernourished we might be during some years, especially when all of our food was rationed.

But growing up in such a family also implied that we were expected to follow the footsteps of our parents, and strive to be the best in learning. Or, in Mom's plain words, "Go to the best schools. Get the highest grade. And get the highest degree possible."

That was the underlying reason for so many things that we did, and the reason for Mom and I taking this particular trip together too.

OUR TRAIN PULLED slowly into yet another stop. We were rushing back to school this time, and had to take this slow train that made many more stops at additional stations. That was why our trip was longer than usual by a few hours. Though at this tiny town in the vast countryside, the planned stop was only for a couple of minutes. Outside of our window, on the narrow platform, there were a few local people trying to sell food and other items to the passengers on the train. A middle-aged lady was making freshly baked pancakes from her old wooden cart. The steam from her mobile stove swirled in the air, brought to us a delicious mixed smell of green onion, cooking oil, and fire.

I took another sip of water and swallowed it down. I wished I could get something warm into my stomach, which felt like a really hard knot for the past few days, especially since we left Beijing yesterday. But to buy any food would cost money. Money that I could no longer ask of my parents. Even though I was sure Mom would not mind buying me a cheap green onion pancake if I did ask. The crisp air outside felt perfect on this early-summer day. Pushed the window up higher, I stuck my head out, feeling the rays of the morning sun on my face. Breathed deep and long, I tried to suck in more of the cooking smell from the stove on the platform, and the heat with it.

"Sit down. We are moving again."

Mom called out to warn me. I pulled myself back inside, and turned to look at her. She was reading her book again. That old pair of round-rimmed, plastic-framed glasses sitting low on her nose, with a piece of white tape holding together the broken bridge in between her eyes. Her short hair framed her beautiful face, dark with silver strands peeking out here and there. Her expression was soft and kind, just as how she always was toward others. Which was why everyone, including most of her students, loved her so much.

But I knew that she was so much more than just kind. She was smart, driven, and strong, with a lot of wisdom. I really should listen to her more. I reminded myself. Mom excelled both in academic and athletic endeavors when she went to college, as one of the few girls in her Engineering Department back in the 1950's. Even though for some of those years, she had to haul dried pancakes and pickled vegetables from home to school twice a year, to sustain herself for months on end at school. She persevered and graduated with honors. Using her own journey as an example, Mom always urged me to strive for the best, no matter what. Especially academically, and that I should aim to "get the highest degree possible."

So I never questioned the significance of an advanced degree, or the reasons behind such a hefty goal. Although I had not done too well with getting that highest *grade* for the most part. But I understood why Mom wanted me to try my hardest. So I could be independent. Especially since I am a girl. The importance of being successful, self-sufficient, and not relying on anyone else was something that Mom drilled in me from very early on.

I loved Mom for all her kindness and strength. Though like any young adult, I did not always heed her advice. Especially since she gave so many of them, all the time. An outsider might even suggest that I went to a boarding school and a university far away from home to test my independence. I really didn't know how much truth there might be in that. As I was not even sure how much of those choices were mine, and not Mom's. Nonetheless, it was a rare treat to travel together with Mom. Last time we made a trip like this, I was only seven. And that tour to visit Mom's hometown and see all her siblings was one that I could never forget.

The train jolted suddenly and started moving again. I looked at Mom and smiled. We were getting closer to our destination, however slow it might be. Secretly, I was also glad that the temptation of warm food was now gone.

Something moved and brushed against my elbow that was resting on the small table. Startled, I almost jumped up. As I turned to look, I saw a grey-colored shadow disappearing through the wide-open window. And something was missing on our tiny table.

"Our lunch box?"

I realized that it was gone now. But how did it just go out of the window? What happened? Forgetting about Mom's warning from earlier, I sat up from the bed, stuck my head and shoulders out of the window once more, and looked back.

As our train labored in gaining more speed to leave the small station behind, I saw a scrawny teenaged boy standing at the end of the platform. He was wearing a shirt that was patched up in several places, and a pair of pants that hang halfway down his calves, edges tattered. He was looking down at something that he held in his hands. Something grey. It was our lunch box, with the buns and the eggs inside. He took our lunch box right out of the window, just as we were passing him by at the station.

My heart jumped into my throat. But there was nothing I could do, except staring at his figure disappearing into the distance. Pretty soon, the entire station was gone from my view.

I sat back down heavily, still speechless and unable to believe what had just happened. I looked back at Mom. She was staring at me, looking aghast. With obvious effort, she closed her mouth. And I realized that my jaw had dropped as well. That boy was fast and skilled. I guessed this was not his first time taking things out of the window of a moving train.

Now we had no more food for the rest of the trip. Although the rubber bands that I took off from the box was still there, sitting lonely and pitifully on that yellow table. Losing the lunch box with our food inside made me remember the hidden container under Mom's pillow, I stretched my hand back again in searching for it.

Mom's hand was already there, grasping the box tight. She was thinking about the same thing, as we both wanted to make sure that *this* lunch box was still there, still inside my school bag, hidden safely. And it was. Mom and I looked at each other, held our hands for a brief moment. And I felt a wave of calm washed over me. Reminded myself to breathe again, I gave her fingers a slight squeeze before Mom pulled her hand out.

Neither of us said anything, but we knew how we both felt – scared and relieved at the same time. I picked up those rubber bands from the table and slid them onto my wrist, as if trying to prevent them from disappearing on me too. I reminded myself that it was just some food that we had lost, and that it was okay. Though it still took me a long time before my heart went back down to where it belonged.

FOR THE NEXT two days, no matter where we visited on the USTC campus, we did not let my school bag or the box inside leave our hands for even a second. Until the third day, when finally it was time for us to go to the accounting office at my University.

Once in front of the line, Mom handed a special form that needed completion to the university accountant who was sitting behind a big desk. Then she took out the tin box from my bag and opened it. From inside the box, Mom revealed a brown envelope and pulled the content from it. Holding that thick stack of cash with both of her hands, Mom stretched her arms out dubiously toward the lady.

Under the watchful eyes of her supervisor standing right behind her, the accountant stood up. She clasped the money from the ends of the stack, and took it from Mom, with a solemn and earnest expression on her face.

She sat back down, put the money on her desk, and started counting the multi-colored hundred-yuan renminbi (or RMB, Chinese currency) bills from it. She counted them twice. Then she looked back at her supervisor, who gave her a slight nod of the head. Satisfied, the accountant opened a drawer and put the money inside. She then found a big official stamp from a different drawer. Inked it carefully on a bright red ink-pad, the lady stamped the paper that Mom gave her earlier, firmly and slowly. Lifting up the stamp carefully, she blew onto the ink to dry it, and double checked.

Mom and I watched the process intensely the entire time, holding our breath without even noticing it. Finally, the lady looked satisfied at the evenly-spread bright red image of the official seal. Her face relaxed and broke into a slight smile. She looked up at us and handed the document back to Mom.

Mom took the paper with both hands, full of apprehension. She examined the stamp carefully herself, before folded the paper up, and put it back into the now empty lunch box. Taking a deep breath of relief simultaneously, we thanked the lady and walked out of their office.

Mission accomplished!

That money had been in our hands for not even seven days.

And what a stressful week it had been.

LATE IN THE afternoon of the previous Friday, at our small apartment home in the suburb of Beijing city, Mom and I anxiously waited for the return of *Gege*. He was going to bring back the money, twelve-thousand-yuan RMB to be exact, for me. Well, actually it was for me to pay my University.

When we heard *Gege*'s key turning in the lock at the front door, I rushed over to greet him, and to make sure that he had the money. Then we walked back together to Mom's bed where she sat waiting. *Gege* took out the same brown envelope from his pants' pocket, thickly filled full with those bills. I couldn't believe that he had just put it in his pocket. But it was Mom who actually voiced her displeasure.

"How could you just put that in your pocket?" She was not very thrilled and made sure that he knew it. "How could you ride your bike with all that money in your pocket? What if it falls out?"

"I was holding that pocket and keeping it safe the entire way home." *Gege* defended himself, putting his hand on the pocket to demonstrate it. The image of him riding his bike came to mind, often with only one hand on the handle, for a long stretch of time. *Gege* was really cool in my eyes. And this skill was one of those things that I always admired about him.

Though Mom's attention had already switched to the stack of cash that she took out from the brown pouch. Making sure nothing was left in there, she cast the empty envelope aside. Then she started counting the bills. For every ten bills she counted, she put them in a separate pile. I double-checked to make sure that there were still ten bills in each pile. Pretty soon, I had to stand up to make room for the last few piles on the bed. When Mom was all done, we all counted the number of piles together.

Twelve piles. Ten bills each. So there were one hundred and twenty bills altogether. Each bill worth one-hundred yuan. The total was twelve-thousand yuan RMB. Exactly as we expected.

"I have never seen this much money in my whole life." Mom muttered quietly. She took out five additional hundred-yuan bills that she had placed under her pillow earlier, adding them into the pack. I looked at her, she was still staring at the money, now stacked back neatly into one thick pile. There was a sense of wonder, a tinge of sadness, and a little bit of envy, all mixed together on her face. I didn't know what to say and stayed quiet.

All of this was for me.

Since I wanted to go to the USA, to further my study, to get that highest degree possible, and to make my parents proud. Before I could go any-where else in the world however, I needed a Chinese passport to be able to leave China. In order to apply for that precious passport, I had to meet stringent requirements from the government, by getting a whole bunch of required forms stamped with those red official seals.

And one of those requirements was to pay back to our universities the tuition that was never charged in the first place. It was a new requirement, added just a few months ago.

Back in the 1980s, all Chinese universities admitted students purely based on one's 高考 scores (*Gaokao*, the infamous China's notoriously tough nationwide college entrance exam). In 1985, when I took the 3-day, 7-subject exam with almost two million other students across the country, colleges picked the applicants with highest *gaokao* scores and nothing else. We, the students, had one chance to list, in priority order, the schools and majors of our choices before submitting our application forms, a few weeks prior to the actual *gaokao* exam. After the exam, we had to wait to see what our scores were, and which school and department accepted us. Once we received the letters with those two pieces of life-altering information, we had no other choice but to attend whichever program we were admitted.

Nobody had to pay a tuition attending schools back then though. Some students from underprivileged families would even get living allowances from the schools to help them out as well. So affordability was really not a main concern for higher education in those day.

But now, the Chinese government simply set an annual tuition amount, and made it a requirement for those who wanted to leave the country after college. And we had to pay back that set amount, for each year that we studied in college, before we were allowed to apply for a passport.

On the flip side, as college professors, my parents received very moderate pay. For many years (during Cultural Revolution), they made a combined monthly income of 120 yuan (less than $20 USD). Though we were still considered as a middle-class family, not bad at all compared to many other families.

So we never had much money. Even though my parents saved as much as they could, our family savings were still not even a fraction of this amount that I needed to pay. In supporting of my efforts to get advanced education overseas, my parents were willing and ready to ask all their relatives and some of their closest friends to borrow their lifetime savings, just so that I could meet this requirement for my passport application.

But I could not fathom putting such a burden on my parents. And put them in debt, financially and emotionally, to all these people that were closest to them. On top of that, the airline ticket alone would take about half of my parents' savings already, not to mention I had to bring something with me to get my life started if I did make it to the US.

So I was determined to find a way myself to pay for this large sum. Luckily, I had this friend, Chengyun, who started his own business while attending college. And by this time, he was already successful enough that he could lend me the entire amount by himself. So I didn't have to rely on Mom and Dad for this enormous sum.

Still, any debt, to anyone, was something that we as a family never had, and a massive burden no matter where that money came from. Was I so selfish that I'd put my family in such a hardship? To that, I had no answer, but I did not feel like I had any other choice either.

BACK TO THE USTC campus. Now that we had paid the University and got the letter stamped to satisfy that particular requirement for my passport application, there was no reason for Mom to stay at my school any longer. She went back to Beijing with the stamped document the very next morning. While I stayed behind to finish all the graduation requirements for my bachelor's degree, and to say goodbyes to my friends, teachers, and classmates.

Those last couple of weeks on campus were a blur: lots of activities, collecting varies graduation-related documents, dinner parties, signing yearbooks, attending our Commencement ceremony, packing up and had everything shipped back to Beijing, etc. Among many other graduation documents that we had to collect and get signed off, a couple of my friends even convinced me to go with them to get an officially-stamped "Pre-approval for getting married" letter from the school HR department.

"Just in case." they coaxed me. As one could not get married legally in China without such an approval. So, I went along, even though Connor, my boyfriend of the last 3 years, and I had not really talked much about marriage.

Very few classmates mentioned where they would be going next though, neither did I, not knowing what to say really. Back in May, I was thrilled to receive an admission letter from New York University (NYU). It informed me that I was accepted into the Ph.D. program in its Biology Department. A subsequent letter from NYU further notified me that they'd offered me a full scholarship in exchange for me working there as a Teaching Assistant.

My family and I were ecstatic for that offer. But, there was still so much uncertainty on whether I could actually make it there, that I had only told a few of my close friends about that exciting news.

Like many others, even though I was putting everything on the line for the goal of attending a graduate school in the USA, the chance was just too slim and it was highly questionable whether it could actually happen. So, as most of my friends, I didn't want to share too much information, with too many others, too soon.

Chapter Two

Back in Beijing, a different kind of busy work started. The last letter from New York University (NYU) suggested that I arrive in New York City (NYC) by the middle of August, a month before school started. So I could get situated and also take the required English as a Second Language (ESL) class for the new Teaching Assistants (TAs), the letter explained.

The middle of August was less than 7 weeks away from the 30th of June, the day when I finally got back to Beijing.

There was still so much to do during this short period of time. I had to register at my new job and set my residency record back to the local municipality in Beijing. Just so that I could get official documents stamped by these agencies as part of the package for my passport application.

Only after I had completed all the pre-requisites, could I then go to the Central Police Station to apply for my passport, my very first passport. If I qualified and obtained that passport, then I would need to go apply for a US entry visa from the US embassy. If I passed that hurdle also, we could finally be certain that I could make it to the US. Then we would move on to the activities like purchasing a ticket for the very first flight of my life. Of course, I would still need to buy and pack what I needed to bring with me, to get medical exams done, to exchange the allowed amount of US dollars for international travelers, and so much more. All before I could get on that plane.

Getting that passport was only the first step. But it was one of the hardest. It was the reason why I had to pay USTC that large sum, and that was just one of the many requirements from the government. I was so envious of *Gege* and Connor (and happy for them), as they were able to get their passports a few months back, before this policy change. Quite a few new requirements were added for all the new passport applicants, like myself, including paying back the tuition to our schools.

Also under this new policy, unless we had a close-relative living overseas, we would not be allowed to apply for a passport, period. Coincidentally, I learned that we had an aunt that lived in the USA. Dad had a verification statement to prove it, with an official government agency stamp on that document too. Though the luckiest people were those who had official paperwork to say that their own parents or grandparents lived overseas, then they didn't even need to pay that lump sum fee to their universities. This was quite ironic as such a relationship with overseas, a decade back during the Cultural Revolution, could land any family in deep political trouble, even jail time or worse. And now it had turned 180 degrees, and became a critical requirement in helping many of us to advance our future.

Thinking back now, decades later, I can understand that the Chinese government did not want to lose too many gifted graduates from the best universities. Especially since college admission was completely merit-based and we did not have to pay tuitions for school. So they tightened the policy to reduce the number of people who could qualify or afford to get a passport. It was a very effective way for China to minimize the loss of talents to other countries. But at that time, I was just so bummed out that I got caught by this change, and that I had to pay so much extra money and do all these extra work to get my passport.

Nevertheless, I was fortunate to be among those who were able to navigate and meet all the new conditions for getting a passport, regardless of the prices we had to pay.

So, as soon as I got back to Beijing, I followed each of the steps under the new regulations, and collected each of the red official seals on all the required documents. By the time we sent Connor off for Los Angeles, at the end of July, I was at the very last step of the process to apply for that precious passport. I was told that I had satisfied all the requirements. So, barring any unforeseen circumstances, they *should* process my application and I *should* be able to pick up my passport on August 7.

I was thrilled with the possibility of becoming one of the few citizens in the entire country with a passport. As Chinese government had *always* been very stringent on who they allowed to travel overseas. Still, the uncertainty weighed heavy in my heart. Until I had that passport in my hands, there was no way that I could relax just yet.

EVEN THOUGH I moved as fast as the process allowed, my schedule was still extremely tight in order to get to New York by mid-August, *if* everything actually worked out. The closest flight on which I could reserve a ticket was on August 18. And that left just ten days between the dates when I could pick up my passport, and when I needed to get on that flight to leave China.

So, everything had to be scheduled right, and well-orchestrated. On August 7, my new passport had to be picked up the very first thing in the morning, and I needed to go to apply for a US entry visa, at the US embassy with that passport, also early in the morning, on the same day.

That would be the date to determine my future.

Would I be able to get that passport without a glitch? Would they grant my visa application at the US embassy for going to NYU?

To be allowed to go to the USA was a dream for many of us. And I certainly wanted to go there to get that *highest-possible-degree* that Mom believed would be crucial for my entire future career and happiness.

Though everyday people around me talked about how slim of a chance it was to actually get approved for a US visa, that only a handful of people would get it each day even though hundreds tried. And it was true from what I had seen. Just a few days ago, *Gege*'s own attempt was rejected, without given any clear reason. But all this talking about how likely we were to fail made my head spin, and I did not want to hear or think about it anymore.

"Let me just try," I pleaded in my head to the universe, "at least give me a chance to try."

Finally, August 7 came.

I got up early that morning, gulped down my breakfast quickly. I put on the clothes that Mom and I picked out together for this special occasion – a clean white shirt, a knee-long blue denim skirt, and a pink sweater that Dad brought back from his trip to Germany a few years prior. Image was important. I needed to dress like a good student to earn a better chance of getting that invaluable visa.

Slung over my shoulder was the same green school bag that I had used for the last five years, which held all the important documents I needed. Mom made sure that my bag was buckled up tight, so I wouldn't accidentally lose anything on my way to the US embassy.

I said goodbye to Mom and left home.

The Embassy District was pretty far from where we lived. I had to change a few buses to get there. By seven o'clock, I arrived at the Embassy Station. The sun was coming up, its light reflected on the newly rain-washed streets. The day started to warm up quickly. Walking toward my destination, I was lost in a very unfamiliar emotion. Feeling adrift as if I was in a thick fog, all by myself, even though the street was getting more crowded by the minute. Many others were headed in the same direction as I was.

It rained hard overnight. And while I was safe and dry in my bed, *Gege* was outside in the rain, because of me. Since yesterday morning, he had been faithfully waiting in a long line outside of the US embassy for visa applicants. He spent all day yesterday, and the whole night last night under his raincoat, keeping that spot in line, for me. So I could have a better chance to step into that embassy building today.

Hundreds of people waited for a chance to go in the embassy each day, to request for a visa to go to the USA. Many came from far away cities and provinces. And most would go home empty-handed. Some would not even be able to step inside the building to present their cases at all. Still, all of us came. With the hope that we could actually get that visa, and be among those fortunate few to be allowed to go to the USA.

I knew for *Gege*, being here again after getting his own rejection had to be especially hard. And I wondered how he felt during the last 24 hours, waiting in that line again, for *me*. What kind of thoughts went through his mind?

GROWING UP, GEGE was perfect in my eyes in so many ways. And he was a great example that Mom always reminded me to follow. His grades were always at the top of his class. He worked hard at school and at his soccer practices. And he could sit for hours at-a-time to read or study. While I often got restless or fall asleep after maybe 15 minutes.

Gege was my teacher, my entertainer, and protector too. I had learned a lot from him, including saving the pennies from our weekly allowance so I could buy something that I really wanted one day.

In some winters after heavy snowstorms, he would find some discarded bamboo planks, tied them to the bottom of a low stool, and made a sled for me to slide down a hillside on the snow. My happy laugh and the fun activity often attracted many other neighborhood kids to join us within minutes.

When I was little, in one summer, he made a battery-powered radio with some electronic parts that he scavenged from Mom's office. And we listened to a comedy talk-show from it when the power went out in the evenings. And whenever I got scared or bullied by a boy, I would scream for *Gege*. His prompt appearances always chased all my troubles away.

Gege had been kind-hearted and very thoughtful toward others, helping people in need when he saw it. He was loved by all the adults and kids alike.

Though *Gege* seemed to always have terrible luck. Whereas I was quite fortuitous to squeak by and enter the schools of my choices by having just high enough scores at those "entrance exams". *Gege*, on the other hand, would repeatedly fail to get accepted himself, even when some other kids with his exact borderline scores were admitted by those schools at random.

We both applied some of the same schools for middle school, high school, and college. And *Gege* never got any break in getting accepted by his first-choice schools. But whichever school he got himself into, he was consistently at the top of his class, and still remained as the role model for me.

And *Gege* always helped me wherever he could without any hesitation or complaint, like waiting in this line outside of the US embassy for the last 24 hours. Though we had no idea if I would face the same rejection today myself. And then what? Just go back to the end of the line and start all over again, if they even let me?

"Oh, stop thinking like this." I told myself, "I should be grateful that I could even get this far this fast."

One thing that really helped me with my quest to go to the USA was the fact that I majored in biology instead of engineering. Following my parents' footsteps, *Gege* studied computer engineering as well. But that major made it a lot harder for him to obtain a full-scholarship from a US university. As a result, he faced a much bigger challenge in getting his visa.

So, I really hoped that my field of study and the full scholarship from NYU would give me a better chance at getting my visa today.

Getting a visa these days was like trying to "win a lottery." A new term that I learned from a friend, Faye. Faye went to the USA last year to attend a school in Los Angeles, across town from the school where Connor just started. Faye and I were best friends since we were five-year-olds. Even though we spent the middle and high school years apart, we reunited at USTC again in the same class 5 years ago. Faye graduated a year earlier to go to the US. And she was one of the main sources for me to gain limited knowledge about life in the US and the schools there.

"You can pay just a couple of dollars," Faye told me about this *lottery* in one of her letters, "to get some lottery tickets, for a chance to win millions of dollars." She marveled.

Though there was a huge difference between getting a US entry visa and winning a lottery. With the lottery, one spent a couple of dollars to buy the tickets, and prayed for the win. Here, we had to work hard for months, sometimes years. We had to spend so much time and money, beg, argue, and plead at all these school and government offices for those critical red stamps. We had to meet all the stringent requirements before we could apply and get our passports, under the ever-changing policies and regulations. And we also had to spend months, sometimes years, applying and praying to get admission and a scholarship from a US school, so we could actually afford to go to the US.

All of this had to be accomplished before we had a reason to come here to the US embassy. To be qualified for a chance to wait through those long days and nights, outdoors without any shelter, regardless of the weather. At the end, most of us would still be rejected by someone who would simply take a look at us, and decided that they didn't feel having someone like us in their country.

And yet we all kept pushing, kept hoping, and kept coming, for that one slim chance of making it. Is that why they called it "the American Dream?" Because for most people, it would always remain just as a dream?

I SAW THE long snake-shaped line of people as soon as I turned the corner from the main boulevard. This was a part of the capital city where we all wanted to come. It felt foreign and mysterious just to be here. The hedges were tall and well-trimmed. The fences were high. The air seemed crispier with an exotic fragrance of unseen flowers. And the architecture with the flags of other nations all seemed to be from another world.

Just being here in this district made us feel like we were already in a foreign land. Sometimes we could also catch people speaking in an alien tongue. Or get a glimpse of someone who had different colored skin, taller nose, bigger eyes, and just looked so different from the rest of us. "洋鬼子." ("Foreign devils.") the elders sometimes called them with distaste. As if they were back in the days when China was occupied by the foreign nations.

But these days, to feel, or actually go outside of the country, the possibility alone was so alluring to so many of us young people. Full of dreams of a different land, a different experience, and a different life, we would go great distances to make it into a reality.

Mindlessly I walked past the families along the waiting line, searching for *Gege*'s dark grey jacket, in hundreds of darkly clothed people. Finally, I found him. Behind just about a dozen others, *Gege* was waiting patiently not far from the US embassy gate. He was visibly relieved when he saw me.

"Is Dad with you?" he asked, at the same time when I asked him, "Is Dad here yet?"

Dad was not yet here. We both fell silent and looked back the way I came from. But Dad was nowhere to be seen.

It was good that they had not yet opened the gate to let people in. We prayed that Dad would get here before we started moving. Dad left home early to pick up my passport that morning. I needed to show the embassy guard my passport before I could be allowed to get inside.

"Why don't you go home and get some rest?" I told *Gege*.

I just remembered how tired *Gege* must be, after such a long wait, through the summer sun and the heavy rain. His eyes were bloodshot and he looked exhausted. "You can go home now. I am good here. And I can wait for Daddy alone." I added.

Neither of us wanted to talk about the possibility that we might have to do this all over again, if Dad didn't get here on time, or he wasn't able to pick up my passport somehow.

"Okay." *Gege* did not argue.

He picked up his still wet raincoat and left for the bus stop. My eyes followed *Gege*'s steps and watched the stream of water dripping off from his coat.

There was a big crowd of incoming flow of people in our direction, but I still couldn't find Dad's familiar face in it.

"Was he able to pick up my passport? Would he be able to get here on time?"

This morning, Dad left home before I even got up, when it was still pitch dark outside. His job was to go to the Central Police Station to pick up my passport and bring it to me at the US embassy. So I could show it to the guard, and be allowed to go inside. We planned all that just so I could get a little more sleep and looked my best when applying for that visa.

"Was Dad able to get my passport? Was he able to get it right after they opened their office? Was there traffic slowing his journey to get here? Could anything else be wrong?"

If Dad wasn't able to pick up my passport, all the waiting *Gege* had done would be for nothing. Even if Dad was able to get that passport, if he got here late, I could still miss my turn at the gate and be kicked out of the waiting line.

The anxious, nervous, tired and unforgiving crowd would be gleeful to see someone else get tossed out. As if that might give them a better chance to get their own visa. And they would not let me to just move a few spots down the line. In that case, we would have to do this whole thing all over again for the next day.

"Maybe I can go straight to the back of this line, and have *Gege* come back later in the evening, to keep that spot for another night."

Not wanting to dwell more on that dark possibility, I occupied myself by double checking all the documents in my bag. I had the acceptance letters from NYU. The I-20 form, which was the document from NYU to the US Immigration Department to certify that I was coming to the US as an international student in their Ph.D. program. The letter from NYU informing me that I was granted a Teaching Assistant scholarship, with a tuition waiver as well as $8,800 a year award in a stipend (this full-scholarship would be a key element in helping me to get that visa). Another letter from NYU suggesting that I came to New York City early. The letter informed me that I needed to attend the ESL class. And my reservation for a flight ticket for August 18, ten days away from today.

From all the reliable sources, we had learned that typically it would take the US embassy at least a week to process a visa, *if* they granted one's request. That would give me just three days to actually purchase my flight ticket; go to the Central Government Bank to exchange that $400 USD allowed for each traveler leaving China; do the medical exams required for foreign travel; terminate my employment; and cancel my residency record in Beijing.

None of these things could be initiated or completed until I showed proof that I had a passport, a valid visa, a purchased ticket, and that I was indeed leaving China. All hinged upon how it would turn out today. Right here at this majestic US embassy.

"Tian Li!" A loud and familiar voice woke me up from my trance. Dad was walking toward me quickly. He was visibly relaxed when he saw me still not yet in front of the embassy guard, though very close already. I was really relieved to see him, and noticed a small item that he held in his hand.

Dad came close, out of breath, and stuffed into my hand a small brown envelope. There was something rigid inside. I opened it, and pulled out a brand new little reddish-brown booklet. It was a passport, *my* passport! With a golden imprint of our national emblem on the cover reflecting the morning sun.

I eagerly opened it up, and saw my picture inside, looking straight back at me. I let out a breath. So far things were progressing smoothly as planned, even though we were really cutting it close.

Now, it was time to see how the next step would turn out.

ABOUT 45 MINUTES after I got inside the Visa Application Office, my name was called. This time, it was from an unfamiliar voice, with a slight foreign accent. It came from Window 6.

Yes! Six is an auspicious number in Chinese culture. Even if I was not superstitious, I was happy to take all the help I could get. I stood up, looked around the large and packed room quickly, to make sure that no one else was responding to that call.

So, it was really for me then.

I wasn't sure what to expect. As I knew that Americans called people by their first names, or at least first names first. But he clearly called "Tian Li" as in our Chinese custom. I guessed that he must have been in China for a while now and followed our culture to call our names.

I walked over to Window 6 promptly. The man sitting behind the glass window looked kind and relaxed. Another good sign.

As he instructed, I passed the I-20 form and my brand-new passport through the opening under the glass window to him and waited.

"Sign your name." My passport came back out.

What? I opened the passport for the second time since I got it this morning, confused.

"Sign your name." he pointed down at the passport.

I looked again. Oh, I needed to sign my name on that passport. Hmmm, how should I *sign* this? Should I write my Chinese name? Should I write in *Pinyin*? I decided to sign in Chinese, wrote my name down on the signature line, and passed it back to him.

"How old are you?" he asked.

"Twenty-two." Even though a lot of people still thought that I looked like a high schooler.

"Where are you going?" he asked again.

"NYU. New York University." I answered.

So far so good. He talked quite slow and clear, in a nice baritone. And he was fairly easy to understand. I remembered the tip to keep my answers as short as possible, and not volunteer any extra information.

The gentleman inside looked through the documents. My heart was beating fast. "What if he ask about that aunt in America?" I thought nervously.

"What are you going to study?" he asked.

"Biology."

"Oh good, no aunt, what was her name again?" my mind seemed to have trouble staying still.

"Who is going to pay for your school?" he looked up, stared at me.

"Ummm. I will be teaching and getting a stipend. No tuition." I got a little nervous under his gaze.

I picked out the scholarship offering letter from NYU and passed it over to him. I was overjoyed when I received that offer, for the generosity of the school. And also because such a "full-scholarship" was believed to really enhance my chance in getting a visa.

"Bai." that was her last name. The aunt that I had not heard of until a couple of months ago. "But what is her first name? What is it? And where does she live in the USA? Ohio? Oh my..." I started to feel my cheeks getting warm, and forced my thoughts to something else.

"It is August 7 already. There are 10 days left before August 18. Ten days only. I need to leave on that flight on the eighteenth. We have made a flight reservation for a seat on that flight. And August 18 is already later than the 'mid-August' suggestion from NYU. I can't be late. Now that I have a chance to meet their timeline, I don't want to be late." My mind was racing and my thoughts were jumping around wildly.

Then I realized that the American sitting on the other side of Window 6, the mighty powerful guy with my entire future at the tip of his pen, had been quiet. He had not asked me any more questions. He was just writing on some paper on his desk. This was my chance. I needed to tell him about my tight schedule. I needed to pick up my visa fast. I needed to get to NYU by the eighteenth.

"Can I pick up my visa this week?" I blurted it out, breaking the silence. It was only Tuesday, maybe he would let me pick it up this Friday? I had rehearsed this phrase in my head several times, to make sure that I would say the right words, and in as few words as possible.

"What?" He was surprised to hear me talking unprompted and looked up again. And then he realized what I had asked.

"I will issue you a visa." he added, as he bent his head down again and resumed writing.

What? Now it was my turn to be taken aback. "What did he say? Oh, he just told me that he will issue me a visa. He is approving my request. I am getting a visa! I am going to the USA!"

Now I realized just how presumptuous I was a minute ago. I was already thinking about the trip. Assuming that he would approve my application, even before he had said anything, while he could have just as easily told me that he would reject it and be done with me.

"Oh, thank you!" I rushed. Pumped myself up with courage once more, I pleaded again, "Can I pick up my visa this week? NYU told me to go next week."

I pulled out the letter from the school, plastered it onto the glass window to show him. And I pointed to the line where it said to be there by mid-August.

He looked at me for a second, "Come back next Tuesday... Next!" He pushed a little thin piece of pink paper through the opening under the window to me.

It was my receipt. My proof of the visa approval. The only proof for all that hard work that we had done up to this point was not for nothing.

And with that, I was dismissed.

Putting the carefully folded pink paper in my bag, I walked out of the US embassy. I felt the energy leaving me, drained. Months of uphill battles, weeks of preparation and rushing around, my entire family had worked so hard for my quest to go to the West. Now it was all paid off, with that little pink receipt.

In just the last couple of hours, I had passed the two most important barriers – getting permission from the Chinese Government to leave China by issuing me a passport, and getting approval to enter the USA from the nice gentleman behind Window 6 by issuing me a visa.

I should be elated. I should jump up and down and cheer. But I just felt drained. Even though I was still very relieved and thrilled that all the prices we had paid would not be wasted. And now the hardest part was finally behind us.

Or, was it?

DAD WAS RIGHT outside, waiting for me. Looking at my face, he grew concerned.

"Did you get it? Are they going to let you go? What happened?" His voice showed his fear and attracted the attention of a few bystanders.

"Oh, no, no problem. I got it. We come back next Tuesday to pick it up." I quickly answered to calm his worries. And his whole face transformed into a big smile.

Suddenly, the crowd shifted and surrounded me as if I had just become an instant celebrity. They were mostly parents like my parents' age. And they were there scouting for any useful information for their own kids' benefits. They moved so close that some of them were pushed against me.

"You got your visa?"

"What did they ask?"

"Where are you going?"

"Which school are you attending?"

"Do you have a scholarship?"

"How much money are they offering you?"

The smile on Dad's face grew even bigger. He proudly stood by me, tried to make sure people didn't press too hard. I answered the crowds' pouring questions, and shared some information with the families who were eager to learn anything and everything.

"When are you coming back to pick up your visa?"

"What does it look like inside the embassy?" ...

The questions were on top of one another, firing like bullets. Envy and eagerness were etched in their voices and poured out of their pores. And it almost felt as if they wanted to suck some of my good *Chi* for their own kids, so they could get their visas as well.

"We need to go now." Dad announced to the growing crowd after a few minutes, "She needs to have some lunch."

And I just realized that it had already passed 12 noon. My stomach had been empty for a very long morning. Like a true hero, Dad parted the crowd to make way for me to leave with him. His workplace was a short bus ride away from the Embassy District. So we went there to eat at their dining hall.

The place was almost empty as the lunch crowd dissipated and people went back to their offices. But Dad was so proud and he told everyone we met that I had just gotten my visa to go study in the USA. He even bought extra portions of pork and green beans for our little celebration lunch.

After lunch, I headed home first, to share the good news with Mom and *Gege*. And Dad stayed behind to finish his work.

Dinner was to be our traditional happy family meal: handmade dumplings by Mom and Dad, from scratch. And I was so looking forward to it. I also wanted to learn more of the details on how Dad got my passport in the morning. And to tell them everything again about what happened inside the US embassy.

But before I had the chance to do that, before the filling for the dumplings was prepared, and the dough was set, I started to vomit.

Chapter Three

I threw up as I never had before. My entire body started to burn and my stomach was on fire. It hurt so bad that I curled up into a ball, not remembering anything about the visa, the passport, NYU, or anything else.

The only thing that occupied my entire body and mind was the iron-hot burning sensation in the pit of my ribs. Hotter than fire, whiter than the sun. It started right inside my stomach, completely consumed my flesh and my mind. And it burned like a white-hot fireball, ever growing and expanding.

Before my mind shut down to allow me to drift into the oasis of a deep though troubled sleep, somehow I remembered what Mom had told me before, "Make sure you cook green beans right. Because some of them can be poisonous if not cooked well..." And remembering all those green beans that I had hungrily stuffed my face with a few hours earlier at lunch.

The next 40 hours I slid in and out of sleep and did not leave my bed the entire time. I remembered waking up to Mom wiping my face with warm towels, putting cool towels on my forehead, and changing them in an attempt to bring down my temperature. The fire in my stomach took a long time to subside. But eventually it did. Leaving behind a quietness of empty, surprisingly light, and a blissful forgetfulness of all the things yet to be done.

By the third morning, I finally got up from my bed and was able to start eating again. Mom made me a small bowl of plain porridge for breakfast. And when that stayed down, she made her signature, delicious steamed egg-cup for my dinner, with light soy sauce and sesame oil dripped on top. Warm and soft, it went down silky smooth and warmed me up from inside.

"You okay to go?" Mom asked gently when I finished the last bit of the warm pudding. She was already dressed in outdoor clothes.

"Go where?" my head was dizzy and foggy. I had forgotten all those tasks that I still needed to complete for my quest to go to the USA.

"Go get your tooth fixed." she reminded me.

Oh, right. Because the short amount of time I had left in China, Mom had to find a dental student who agreed to do me a favor by fixing a molar that had a sizable cavity, on such short notice.

"Sure." I answered weakly.

Gingerly I stood up and realized just how sluggish I felt. Though I did not believe I had a choice but to go. Slowly, I changed, picked up my jacket and left our apartment, holding onto Mom's arm.

By the time we got to that dental school, the sun had already set. We found the future dentist in a dark room, with her boyfriend, waiting for us. I learned that the boyfriend was my Mom's student. And that was how Mom was able to find her to help me out that night.

The room was so dim that it was hard to tell if this was a small classroom, an office, or an actual dental treatment place. In the middle of the room, there was a small lamp lit up a chair in which I was told to sit.

I sat down on the chair. And the dentist inspected my impacted molar. She told us that it would be much better to just pull it out, rather than trying to fill the cavity. The hole was too large, she explained, and I didn't have the time, nor her the skills, to get a crown. Mom told her to proceed. Although none of us could have anticipated just how long and difficult that procedure was going to be.

It was a huge blessing for me as my head was still in a dense fog from the food poisoning. I do not recall if they had used any anesthesia to numb the area. The only thing I remember, decades later, is that she said the molar had to be broken up first before its extraction.

But what a stubborn tooth that was.

Onto the long chisel rod that she placed on the tooth, she, and later on, her boyfriend, hammered down hard with a fat mallet. But that tooth stayed intact, while my head jerked back into the seat with each blow, into that unsteady dental chair.

I kept sliding down in that chair. Maybe it was the plastic cover on the chair made it extra slippery. Or it was my body's feeble attempt to escape the torture. I didn't know. Though pretty soon, the boyfriend started cursing under his breath after each of his unsuccessful attempt, sweat beaded up on his forehead.

With the dentist's face next to his, they looked intently into my mouth, after each blow, which was increasingly forceful. They looked and hoped for a crack in the tough enamel. Her face was flushed. And I started to doubt if Mom had made the right call to agree on pulling that molar out, as obviously it did not want to leave my jaw.

I should consider myself very fortunate that the boyfriend was there to help. He was much stronger and he hammered down much harder. Eventually, in what felt like hours later, the tooth finally gave in and broke into two halves. But the dentist cheered a little too soon.

The next step of her using a pair of large extraction forceps to clamp onto the broken pieces, twisting, turning, and pulling in order to get each piece out seemed to be no less of a conquest. Pretty soon, she started to shoot pleading looks to her beloved boyfriend again.

By this time, my Mom's engineering student was hooked on the initial success of his own very first dental job. He volunteered to do the honors again. He yanked hard on those remains of my poor tooth.

My mouth was stuffed full of cotton balls. Replaced quickly each time when they were filled up by heavy-metal tasting blood. The soaked cotton balls got dropped into a basin sitting on the floor.

When that long night's work was finally done, despite the pain and suffering, I cheered in my head. The ordeal was over at last. Mom's student was the one who got the job completed. He stood there, proud and satisfied at his handy work, after he dropped the halves of the tooth into the same bucket.

Our future dentist, his girlfriend, looked up at him, full of awe and admiration on her face. I was left trying to nurse my sore jaw and clamping down on the new cotton balls filling that gaping hole where the tooth used to be. And Mom, full of concern on her face, was also relieved that we were finally finished.

When Mom and I left that dental office, late that night, I had to lean on Mom's arm even more. At the bus stop, Mom bought me an icicle treat from the ice cream lady selling from the back of her tricycle icebox. As the dentist suggested to use that to cool my mouth and to stop the bleeding faster. Eating that frozen juice bar with a big cotton ball inside my cheek was not an easy task, but I thoroughly enjoyed the cool sweetness as I held the icy cold liquid in my mouth.

It was already near ten o'clock. When we stepped onto that last bus of the night, a crowd filled up quickly behind us. It was a group of black guys, who just got out of the university. One of them caught my eye, looked down on my juice bar, and exclaimed,

"Hey. That looks good."

I tried to smile to be polite, but my swollen face did not budge. So I just looked at him, saying nothing.

"Are you a student?" he asked me, thick with an accent of unknown origin. Seeing my quizzical face, he repeated his question again, slowly he said, "Are - you - a - student?"

I nodded my head, feeling the throbbing of my cheek, probably half times bigger than my other side still, a little embarrassed.

"Did you understand what he said?" Mom asked me after we got off the bus.

"He asked if I was a student." I spit out the cotton ball, finally starting to get my mouth back.

THE NEXT FEW days went by fast. I got to eat as many dumplings as my stomach could take. I was pretty sure Mom and Dad wished that I could eat enough in those few days - my last days in China - to sustain me for the rest of my life, if that was possible.

Every day I had a long list of things that I needed to get done. There were more documents to be filled out, signed, and stamped. I had to get required physical exams and additional immunizations. We needed to purchase additional items that I needed to bring to the US. In the evenings, I visited my teachers and older relatives to inform them that I was leaving. And we received many others who came to visit me to bid their farewells.

Also, we started to pack.

Dad had his own methodology on a lot of things. But he was especially proud of his packing skills. In fact, he was so proud that he declared nobody could put anything more into a suitcase that he packed, including himself. It looked like an impossible number of things that he neatly piled into the suitcases, explaining as he did for my benefit.

"Rigid shaped items need to go in after a layer of cloth that has already made the bottom flat," he demonstrated, and "then you stuff the small items into and around it."

He explained as he put a mid-sized cooking pot onto a layer of bedsheets, added some thin clothes at the bottom of the pot. Then he put a smaller saucepan inside the larger one, and stuffed rolled shirts and skirts into the small pan and in the gap between the two pots.

"Put the lid on after you fill up the pot..." he showed me, "upside down, so its knob won't stick out and take up more room."

He wrapped the big chopping knife with a hand towel, put it under the pots. He then put a soapbox next to the handle of the knife, and filled the inside of the soapbox with socks.

"Wear the heaviest boots and coat onto the plane." he advised me, even though it was the middle of summer. "It could get cold on the flight. And it won't take up space inside the suitcases."

"Bring this soft blanket with the tiger-face-print on it. It will protect you in your sleep." Dad folded the blanket over itself twice and lined it up to the inside of the suitcase's top cover.

"Take this hat too." He pulled a baseball cap from a protective bag. I knew that cap. It was one of his favorite items. He got it from this American car company, Cadillac, when he took a group of engineers there to visit a couple of years back.

"Americans like this kind of hat." Dad explained. My heart felt warm by his generosity for giving me such a beloved item of his own.

"The dictionaries are heavy, so you should put them at the bottom of the suitcase. You need two dictionaries?"

I nodded. A general one and a biology one, I needed both.

"Okay, put them side by side, spine against spine. So you don't bend the pages inside."

Watching Daddy pack the suitcases was like a show that I could never get tired of. It was almost like a class that I wished the universities would teach, loaded with so much wisdom from his years of experience.

Dad was super smart.

He grew up in a remote village in the mountains of 五台山 (Wutaishan). When he was a teenager, his father told him to quit school and to become a carpenter like himself. Dad rebelled. My grandfather chased my Dad with a big wooden stick in his hand, threatening to break my Dad's legs so he couldn't go to school anymore. Dad ran. And he kept on running, away from home. He ran to his school that was few kilometers away. And he lived there for years, before he applied and got into the best engineering program in the country – at Tsinghua University. He became a legend in his county because of that achievement.

Later, Dad was sent overseas for a graduate degree. After returning to China, he was hired into the Department of Engineering at USTC, soon after the school was founded. A school that I liked to compare to the University of Oxford or MIT, however biased I might be.

A few years later, Dad rose to be the chairman of the Engineering Department at USTC. Though he had to leave the academic world altogether when we moved back to Beijing.

Dad was funny, witty, and most of all, he loved me dearly. When I was growing up on USTC campus as a kid, I felt like everyone in the University knew him, and at least half of the people knew that I was his "掌上明珠"

(little pearl in his palms). He often carried me around on his shoulders at gatherings, and I spent a lot of time in his office while he worked.

"How many pairs of chopsticks do you need?" Dad's question brought me back to the task on hand.

"Four?" I didn't know why I would need more than one pair. But just in case, I figured.

"Want a spoon too?" he asked.

"Yeah."

In fact, I had already brought all these items, or maybe Mom did, to the packing area, which had taken up the entire space on their bedroom floor and their bed. But Dad needed to go over them himself. And he would let us know if he didn't think it was enough, or that if it was too much.

"Pillow?" he asked again.

Hmmm, this, I was not sure. Obviously, I would need a pillow. But that could take a lot of space. Plus, buckwheat-filled pillows that we used in China were also pretty heavy. And we needed to keep these suitcases within their weight limits.

"Maybe just the pillowcase, two of them. I will buy a pillow when I get there."

We always needed "doubles," so we had something to use while waiting for one to air-dry after being hand-washed each time.

Mom went to the family's big wooden storage chest where she kept all her treasured textile items, and came back with two brand new pillowcases.

"How pretty." I exclaimed. The material was super soft to the touch too. "How come we never get to use them when we are home?"

The packing exercise took place almost every night. In and out, out and in, over and over again. Each time after Dad was done, the extra foot of material would somehow magically disappear into the suitcases.

"The key," Dad told me, "is to use your body weight to press the cover down so you can close it."

And he would demonstrate it as he pressed down hard with his knee on top of the cover. He would shift his weight over the suitcase, before locking and zipping the cases shut.

As I watched him laboring on the closure, I always envied that he weighed so much more than I did. "How could I ever get that done by myself?" I doubted in my head but decided to push that useless question out of my mind.

And when he was done, breathing hard as if he had just run a 3,000-meter race, Dad would smile triumphantly. And whether he said it or not, I knew that he was proud of what he had just accomplished – an impossible endeavor.

Chapter Four

On one such occasion after he closed the suitcases, and weighted them (both within a few grams from the weight limit set by the airline), Dad sat down next to me on the bed. Taking my hand in his, he became quiet. I sensed that he had something important to say, so I waited.

Very quietly, he asked me, "Do you really want to go to America?"

I was shocked by the question. But I could tell that he was serious. After all that we had done, did I really have a choice? I didn't respond.

He spoke again, "It's okay if you don't want to go."

Stunned. I couldn't believe that he was giving me a way out.

For months, no, for years, like many of my friends, instead of relaxing or spending time to have fun, I had prepared, applied, studied, and took tests, for this goal of going to the USA. I took the TOEFL (Test of English as a Foreign Language), GRE (Graduate Record Examination), and the GRE subject tests. I researched the schools and the processes. I asked for recommendation letters from my professors. I spent almost all my allowances on these exams and school application fees, for those schools that wouldn't waive it for me. And I asked my parents for more money when my savings ran out.

I borrowed money to pay the University. We found this aunt in the US. And there was so much more. The whole family, and many relatives and friends, including Chengyun, and that engineering student of Mom's and his dentist girlfriend, all had been sucked into this vortex of tasks, a massive operation, at so many levels.

Plenty of people worked tirelessly, just for me, to help me succeed, to get me to where I was now. So, I could go to the USA, and go after that high degree of academic achievement that was so critical to my future.

And to think of it, the reason that I had left Beijing to go to USTC for college, in the small and remote city of Hefei, was mostly because it was said that USTC sent most of its graduates abroad. And the name itself, it was not only University of Science and Technology of China, but the acronym also came to jokingly stand for the "US Training Center."

It was one of the toughest schools to get into. And biology was one of the hottest departments at USTC.

Before *gaokao*, and before I officially submitted my college application, we had already seen in the public posting that USTC would only accept *one* student from all the applicants in Beijing city into its Biology Department. We all thought Mom was crazy by adding biology at USTC as my very first choice on that application form. It happened the night before the submission deadline. And she moved engineering to be my second choice. When I handed the form in the next morning to my home-room teacher (who taught us math and also took care all of our academic and non-academic related issues for three years), he had shaken his head for Mom's unrealistically ambitious expectations.

Luckily (for Mom and for me), I performed unexpectedly well at the *gaokao exam*. My score turned out to be the highest among all the USTC biology applicants in our city. So, I took that lone spot.

On my first train ride to USTC, without knowing, I sat across from someone who had gone to a different department in our school. He actually hated me for taking "his spot," as his first choice was biology as well. And his *gaokao* score was only 6 points lower than mine.

Okay. Maybe I was willing to go farther away and to live more independently after high school, so I didn't mind to apply for a school that was a long distance away from Beijing. But there were plenty of other outstanding schools outside of the capital city. And I certainly did not need to go after the most competitive program in the entire county.

I knew the reason that Daddy asked that question was not because he doubted the decision for me to go to the USA. It was because he loved me too much to tolerate the idea of sending me so far away, all by myself, and we didn't even know when we may see each other, if ever, again.

Just think about it. If it took my parents nearly thirty years to save up to less than a thousand dollars in total, when would we be able to even afford another ticket to fly across that ocean? And how would we be able to get another visa to do that?

We both knew that the commitment for me to go to the US was already made a long time ago. And that even if Daddy was willing to give me a way out now, it was no longer a real option.

But I didn't know what to say or how to respond to his question. I just nodded, and told him,

"I know. And yeah, I still want to go."

LATER THAT NIGHT, Mom, Dad and *Gege* went out. And I was alone in the apartment. I pondered on Daddy's question again.

"Why *am* I going to the USA? When was that decision even made? Was it 5 years ago when I (I mean Mom) completed that college application form, when I was only 17? Why am I leaving China now? What do I want from this venture? Why have I gone through hell, put my family through hell, to get here? Just so that I can leave all the people I love, all the things I know, the city and the country that I love, and literally leave everything behind? Except for the cooking pots that I will bring, and the chopsticks, the chopping knife, the pillowcases, some clothes and shoes, blankets and sheets, and some dictionaries. I am leaving everything and everyone that I ever had and ever knew, to go to a place that I know almost nothing about, to a city that I have only seen in the movies. And most of the time, not even in a good light: with violence, dirty and scary subways, dark and steaming alleys of the Chinatown and its gangsters and gunfights."

So why was I so determined to go to a place like that still? Why was it that I had no doubt in my mind that I *would* go? Even when I had no idea what my life would be like over there at all?

Was it because the smiling faces of the students from the brochures that NYU sent me looked so cheerful and free? Was it because the grass in Greenwich Village looked so lush and the flowers so pretty? Was it because the Washington Square Arch that I was confused at first with the Arc de Triomphe in Paris looked so mighty? Or was it because of the money that NYU said that they would pay me, $8,800 a year, which was many times of my parents' combined income already?

And the boy I loved, Connor, the only guy I had ever dated and kissed, had left for the USA himself. Though in the midst of all the tasks on hand, sending him off was just one teary moment that was quickly replaced by all the other things that I had to think about and deal with. Since he was in Los Angeles, I would still be on my own in New York City.

So, why was I so determined to go?

I did not have an answer.

I closed my eyes and tried to imagine what my life would be like, if I stayed in China.

In my mind's eye, it would be like the 长安街 (Changanjie). The longest and widest boulevard through the heart of Beijing city, centered right in front of 天安门 (Tiananmen) Square. Like an axis of the city, it went straight for many kilometers in both directions. And if somehow you got the shotgun seat on a bus (as one of the favorite things we liked to do when we were little), you could see so far down that street, as if it would take you to the end of the world. No twists or turns, no surprises, nothing hidden, all clear as day. And just like the view on that boulevard, my life in China would be very predictable, plain, and straight forward.

I already had two dream job offers.

One in a prestigious research institute, under the Chinese Academy of Science. And the other, a job in a very promising startup company, right at the heart of 中关村 (Zhongguancun, later dubbed as "China's Silicon Valley"), in Beijing's 海淀区 (Haidian District, aka, the "College District" where so many of the best high-tech businesses in China were starting at that time). I knew my parents would find a well-suited boy to match me up if Connor and I couldn't work out at the end (if I let them), and they would also make sure that my career progression would be as smooth as it could possibly be, as long as I did a decent job on my end.

I could see my entire life played out in front of my closed eyes. It would be unburdened, uneventful, easy, and predictable. And yet, I was certain that it was *not* what I wanted.

And what could I see, after a pause, when I tried to switch my thoughts to imagine what my life would be like in the USA?

Try as hard as I could with my wildest imagination, the only thing I could see, was a white and dense fog. A fog that was impenetrable, unmoving, unyielding, thick to the point that a knife could cut through it.

It reminded me one foggy morning when I was very little, maybe only four years old. We had just settled down after our move to Hefei. And our family of four lived in a small room that used to be a student dorm, in a dorm building with other families like us.

That morning, in that tangibly thick fog, I sat outside, on top of a tall pile of wooden logs for some construction project. I held my hands out in front of my face, and I couldn't see my own fingers even though they were right there wiggling around.

The log was bumpy and hard, not at all comfortable to sit on. I was there regardless. Even though I had no idea how I got there. I sat next to some other kids from our building. *Gege* must be there too. An older boy was telling us a scary story, of some ghosts of a sort.

I was scared by the story, uneasy on my seating, blinded by the fog, but unable to move. I was afraid that if I tried to leave or stand up, I might fall off from that tall pile.

Just like in that fog, life in America seemed to be a complete mystery to me. It was uncomfortable to even think about, and maybe a little scary too. I had no clue where to start to guess what it might be like. And yet, I had no doubt in my mind that it was the road that I wanted to travel on. I wanted to see what was behind that heavy and impassable fog.

EVEN THOUGH IT had only been a few days, it felt like a century had passed since I first set foot into that embassy building. I went back to pick up my passport with the new visa inside, on Tuesday, August 14.

With that little pink receipt in my hand, I passed through the security at the embassy gate and entered into the building again, without having to wait in line this time. I felt the inquisitive, suspicious, and envious looks from those people waiting, and remembered that I was in their position only a few days ago myself.

I was quite relieved when I got my passport back, and glad that I could finally hold it in my hands to inspect it closely without feeling rushed. My passport picture showed an expressionless and emotionless face. And I wondered what was going through my mind when it was taken, or was I thinking of anything at all?

The visa, instead of a red stamp as I expected, was brightly colored. I was not sure whether it was glued or printed on that passport page. But it took the space of an entire page with a background of a beautiful picture. I admired every single detail of that little booklet and read every line on it, especially the visa itself. It felt as if it came from that far away and mysterious land of the USA directly.

And I was very surprised when I found a number "2" printed on the "Number of Entries Allowed" line. Two? I thought everyone got just one entry if they got approved at all. How come I got two? It was not as if I would use the second entry. Why should I? Because that would mean that I had to leave the USA before I would need to go back in again, within the 6 months window. There was zero chance for that to happen. I almost felt guilty as for sure I would waste such a wonderful gesture that nice gentleman behind Window 6 gave me. But I lent no more thought to it. I was going to the USA. And *that* was all that mattered.

After I got home that night, I called the only person we knew at New York University, Wendy. Wendy was a super smart girl whose dad actually taught my Dad in his high school. Wendy herself went to USTC when I was still in the elementary school there. And she had been working toward her Ph.D. degree at NYU for a few years now.

On our call, Wendy asked me a few questions about my planned trip, the date, flight number, and what I had arranged once I got there. To that last question, my answer was a vague "Ahhh ... I don't know ... I am sure the school had thing arranged."

I had no idea how it would work at all. But all the boarding schools I attended had assigned lodging for us before we got there. So I would expect NYU to be no different.

Wendy was quiet for a minute and then she offered to find someone to pick me up from the airport when I arrived, as she no longer lived in New York City, or even close to it. I thanked her for the foresight, and realized that I had not even thought about *anything* beyond getting on that flight to go to America.

"Oh well, it's only four days away. There isn't enough time for me to write to the school and ask. So, I will just have to wait to find out when I get there." I dropped that train of thought quickly, and got busy again on the things that I had to take care of before my flight.

Now that I had confirmed and could provide prove that I was indeed going to the USA, the rest of the work had to be completed in order, in the last 3 days of my time in China.

The airline ticket had to be confirmed and purchased. Additional immunization and medical exams for international travelers had to be done. I needed to officially resign from the company that I never actually worked for. My residency in Beijing had to be canceled. And I also could finally go to the Central Bank to exchange that maximum-allowed $400 for each verified international traveler. Even though I had no idea where my parents got that money from, after we had just spent several thousand yuan to purchase my flight ticket.

And sprinkled into all these important tasks, we continued to pack and have all those farewell gatherings with many others.

Last night in Beijing, the night of August 17, when the last of the visitors were finally gone, Dad packed my suitcases one last time. After he closed the large cases, he bound them tightly with luggage straps. We weighed them again, both still within their weight limits. Dad stood them on their sides, and put them in the hallway, ready for my journey the next day.

It was past mid-night when we were done with all the preparation, and finally time to go to sleep. I sat on my bed, the bed that I had only stayed in during school breaks for the last 11 years. Now I had no idea if I would ever sleep in it again. I brushed my bedsheet with my hands to smooth out the wrinkles. When my hand reached the pillow, I remembered my diary hidden under it. I had not had time to write in there since I got back to Beijing. I took that red notebook out. I had only written about 10 pages in there so far. Wishing that I had documented more of my unusual experience of the last few weeks, I put it inside my small suitcase.

"I will write more when I get to the USA." I promised myself.

By now, it felt like I had done everything I could think of. Although other than the call with Wendy, and knowing that she would send someone to pick me up at New York airport, I had no idea about anything else on what was waiting for me in America.

"But it is time now. The fog is descending upon me. And the rest is nothing that I know or could do anything about tonight. I will just have to deal with it when I get there. Tomorrow, I will be on my way. I will find out soon enough what is indeed on the other side."

I thought as I turned off the light, laid down, and drifted into a dreamless sleep.

WESTBOUND

It is during our darkest moments that we must focus to see the light.

~ Aristotle

Chapter Five

August 18, 1990

The departure day had finally arrived. After all the rushing-around, all the trips to different agencies to get me to this point, and all the goodbye meetings with friends and relatives in the last couple of weeks, it felt like I had nothing left to do, and nothing left to say. The hour-long drive to the airport was surprisingly relaxed and quiet.

Beijing airport looked familiar, yet, different. I had been there a couple of times before, always sending people off to foreign countries, to those mysterious places that I knew almost nothing about. After each send-off, I would go back to my normal life and do my normal things. And now, it was my turn to leave. My turn to go into that tunnel-of-no-return. And my turn to actually find out what laid beyond, on the other side.

Saying goodbye to my family was quite different this time too. In the last years, I had left home plenty of times when I headed back to my schools, especially to my college. We usually bid our goodbyes on the platform at the train station. But this was different. This time, I was going to a place where we didn't have *any* known friends, in a different country. And we did not even know when we might see each other again.

Though what I did know was that there were several friends of mine who had already embarked on such journeys, and went to the USA. And if they could do it, there was no reason that I couldn't.

A couple of my younger cousins came along as well. They also wanted to go to the US when they graduated from college. I promised them that I would write letters and tell them about my experience in the USA and help them where I could. They helped *Gege* in taking care of the heavy suitcases and getting them off from the rented van. They found a cart to put the luggage on, and wheeled them to the ticket counter for me.

Though none of us talked too much. I carried my brand new, much bigger, red-colored canvas messenger bag – my new school bag. It was slung across my shoulder, with all my important documents inside. Mom had sewed close a pocket in my pants, with that four hundred dollars sealed inside, tucked safely against my skin.

We waited in the long line for checking in at the ticket counter. It looked like all the other families were excited about their trips, while we seemed to have trouble finding new topics to talk about. Mom reminded me several times, "Write to us if you can't call." I just nodded each time, not trusting that I could talk and not cry. When our group finally got to the front of the counter, I held my breath as they weighed the luggage. Well, Daddy certainly did an excellent job packing all that stuff in, and neither piece went over the weight limit.

My ticket, passport, and the visa on the passport, were all in good order. I got my boarding pass without any issue. Now it was time to say our final goodbyes.

Holding the handle of my small suitcase, I got into the back of the line for all the waiting travelers. Mom held my hand and seemed to be reluctant to let go. It looked like she was about to say something again. But I nodded quickly before she opened her mouth.

"Yes. I know. I will try to call, and I will definitely write." I reassured her.

Dad broke his silence, "Study hard! Do a good job!"

I smiled at him weakly, "Thanks Dad, I will miss you too."

And then I looked at *Gege* and my cousins. "I will let you know what it is like over there." *Gege* simply nodded his head.

I turned around, eyes stinging. But I held my tears back. I would miss my family so much. But this was not the time nor the place to think about that. This was the beginning of my adventure to go through that fog, to go see what lies beyond, and to go to the USA.

The line moved swiftly. Pretty soon, I was on the other side. Looking back one more time, I was shocked to see Mom wiping her tears away. She had never cried sending me off before. In fact, I didn't remember her ever crying, not even when she was curled up from pain before her surgery when I was younger.

Once through the customs though, the grey dividers completely blocked any view from where I had come, and where my family was when I last saw them.

"OK! It's all me now." I told myself.

Taking a deep breath, I looked around, tried to figure out what to do next. The airport was huge and very crowded, with more foreigners than I had ever seen. People were walking in all different directions. Some seemed to be in a big hurry while others looked to have too much time to kill.

Somehow in this crowd, I felt lonelier than I had ever been. I didn't know anyone, didn't know what I should do, or where I should go.

"Oh. I will just have to figure it out."

Pumping myself up, I looked around. I saw a small crowd of people in front of a cluster of TV monitors, and joined them there to find where this "gate" for my flight was.

TWO HOURS LATER, I stepped onto our plane, the first plane that I had ever set foot on. I looked around and was quite impressed. It was spacious, nice and clean inside this giant metal bird. Much wider than a train, and seemed taller too. There were a few charming and courteous flight attendants greeting us and showing us the way to our seats.

All the seats faced forward, like rows of soldiers in uniform. The seat cushions were covered in grey cloth, almost like sofas, nice and soft. They all had seat belts and armrests.

"Wow! Airplanes are so different than the trains. It looks incredible. The seats look so much more comfortable than the hard seats on the trains, too." I thought. Everything was so new and wondrous. I was excited about this adventure ahead.

But our take-off got a little shaky and scary, and our flight was jolted by quite a stretch of turbulence. By the time we landed at our first stop, Shanghai airport, I had already thrown up twice. I realized then that this trip may not be all glorious and pleasant as I had imagined. To come down and land at Shanghai airport, we had to dive through some dense clouds. That was not enjoyable at all. It also meant, I dreaded, that we would have to go back up through the same clouds again in a couple of hours.

So, air travel was not all charming and exciting. My stomach did not like it. My head started to hurt as well. And I was only a few hours into this trip, with more than twenty hours ahead. A 13-hour flight to San Francisco was next. And after a short break there, we would fly another 5 hours to go from San Francisco to LaGuardia Airport in New York City.

And apparently, none of these airports' authorities seemed to trust whichever airport we just came from. They each had to make sure that they saw, checked, and weighed our luggage themselves before they let us recheck them through customs.

AFTER THE LONG flight to San Francisco, my curiosity and excitement about finally being on the US ground were waning fast. I was fighting a losing battle with my tired body and mind. I just passively followed the crowd, trying to stay close to those who were also headed to LaGuardia. We didn't have a lot of time at this airport, and the prospect of getting back into another suffocating flying steel-box was grim.

"Oh well, one last leg," I told myself, "and the trip will be over."

But my checked luggage showed up late on the conveyor belt. By the time I got through the customs, I could see that my luck of the last few weeks had been turned upside down. In spite of my feeble prayers, I got picked to wait at the end of the line for detailed inspections. The inspector in front of us looked quite grumpy. He seemed to be determined to share whatever misery he was feeling by making the process extra long and tedious. I waited in distress, envious of others who zoomed through the other lines quickly.

Finally, it was my turn. I was instructed to put all my suitcases and bag, large and small, onto the giant steel examining table. It took all my energy and strength to get them hoisted up.

"Open them." The inspector held a little stick and waved it over my suitcases.

"Open my suitcases? *All* of them? Oh no." I screamed in my head. Although I tried to swallow those words inside, planned to follow his order swiftly. So maybe he would be pleased by my willingness to collaborate and let me go sooner.

Though when I looked down at my giant suitcases, it felt like there were trapped, caged, and vicious giant beasts in there. They had been crammed up and whacked around by the long and bumpy voyage, and couldn't wait to be let out. I felt that they would roar to life once I opened those two containers, and nothing in this airport would be able to tame them back down again.

"All of them?"

I had to ask. I had to try. My eyes pleaded at the inspector. He looked at me, cold, expressionless. And he pointed his little stick onto each piece of the luggage emphatically and deliberately, as he opened his mouth again,

"All - of - them." he repeated, slowly and clearly.

I gave a resigned sigh and started to open them. I untied the luggage straps, unzipped and unlocked the suitcases, and laid the covers on their backs. As soon as they were open, I watched in dismay at the oozing of the contents out of the confines of the containers and spilled right onto the table. Inside, I cringed at the idea of how I could shove them all back when this nightmare was over.

But the inspector was in no hurry. He tapped randomly at items still inside.

"What's this?"

"What's in this pot?"

"What's under it?"

"Take this out."

"Open this."

"And this... and this... and that..."

Everywhere his stick went, my eyes followed and my hands flew over. So I could uncover whatever he wanted to see, and to show him that I had nothing to hide.

At this point, I just wanted to make him happy so I could get this done quickly. When he was satisfied with the content in the first suitcase, he moved on and did the same thing for the second one.

I pulled out my blanket, my clothes, even socks and underwear. I took out the cooking pots, the chopping knife, my pillowcases, the dictionaries. All were laid out for the entire world to see. My face was burning red, how embarrassing.

But this inspector did not care. He lazily flicked through the items with his stick. As if his mission was to isolate every item, at the slowest possible pace. Every few seconds, he would take a break of some sort to look around, like he wanted to make sure that his colleagues knew he was working. And if there was ever a contest for slowest inspection, I was certain that he wanted to win the gold medal with the world record. He definitely did not care about my obvious anxiety, or maybe he just really wanted to torture me. I had no way of knowing.

Out of the corner of my eye, I saw the last passenger from my flight disappearing along the next long corridor. I was now left behind, alone, as the only passenger from our plane that was still stranded there.

When the inspector had finally had enough, he waved his stick in the air and dismissed me. Then he turned and walked away, leaving me to deal with the aftermath alone.

In front of me, on the large steel inspection bench, besides my opened carry-ons, my two giant suitcases laid bare. They were spread out like slaughtered animal remains, with all their glorious insides spilled around. All Dad's carefully folded and packed items undone. The fierce eyes of the tiger on that soft printed blanket laid crooked, staring at me, looking so sad and tired somehow.

I rushed to stuff everything back into the cases, not paying attention to how and where they would fit. I ignored Dad's instructions that insisted on playing in my head about the "right ways" of packing. The content piled almost twice as high as the suitcases themselves. I had to try to close them by using my own little stick of an elbow and all my feeble power. I tried to apply whatever pressure I could muster onto these cases that were placed on the waist-high inspection tables.

Sweat started to bead up on my face, and trickle down my back, under the thick overcoat that I was wearing. As I tried to zip close and lock the cases, I thought how unfair it was that Dad had the huge advantage when he closed them at home. As he could use his strong knees and all of *his* body weight to accomplish the final closure, on the concrete floor in our Beijing apartment. And here I was, trying to flop as much of my upper body as possible onto the cases, just to add a little more weight to try to close that big gap.

When I actually zipped the last case shut, I was more surprised than proud. And after I moved the cases back onto my cart, I realized my error. There, on the now empty steel bench, my cooking pot was left alone. Without a lid, it looked like a fish that was dead on the beach, with its huge mouth wide-open, gaping vast and lifeless.

No wonder I could close the cases, I thought. And no, I would not leave anything here at this airport. Not after we spent so much money, time and energy to carefully select and pack these items in Beijing. And I was not going to leave my precious cooking pot to this terrible inspector. He would not win.

I looked around. Obviously, I was not going to open back up any of my suitcases to try to fit the pot back inside. So the only option I saw was to somehow stuff it into my red messenger shoulder bag.

I opened my red bag all the way up, tried to fit the pot inside. Though only the bottom of the container reluctantly sank in. With its top half sticking out, it threatened to jump out at any moment.

That would have to do, I decided. I laid my left hand and forearm onto the handle of the luggage cart to push it forward, while holding on to the opening of my red bag with my right hand, to make sure nothing would fall out from the fully opened pouch.

With that, I pushed hard and ran as fast as I could. With my red bag bouncing on my hip, I ran in the direction of the last passenger.

WHEN WE FINALLY arrived at LaGuardia Airport, I didn't think I had anything left in me. Everything I tried to put into my stomach in the last thirty plus hours had come back up and out. But I was finally here. My destination. New York City. No more flights. No more inspections. No more turbulence. I just hoped that Wendy's friend would be able to identify herself and find me, as I followed the crowd, making my way outside.

As soon as we came out of the door, a sea of receiving people appeared in front of us. There were so many sets of eyes looking at us, eagerly scanning every passenger coming through those doors, in searching for their loved ones. Quite a few people stared at the strange sight of my cooking pot sticking out of my shoulder bag, as I was still trying to hold on to them while pushing my heavy cart with the other arm. Loud cheers came left and right as families reunited. I tried to listen to the names being called out, in searching of mine from the raucous noises, but none came.

I started to wonder just how Wendy's friend, whom I had never met, would be able to find me in such a crowded place, when I noticed a group of Chinese students among those waiting. They held up some paper signs, with Chinese names written on those signs. There were a whole bunch of them, all boys though, with many signs held in their hands.

I walked closer. And there, my name was on one of those signs. I walked over to the person holding it, pointed at my name, and looked into an unfamiliar face.

"Are you Tian Li?" he asked.

I nodded, "Yes."

"OK, wait behind us." he told me. He glanced quickly at my cooking pot but did not comment on it. He gave me the piece of paper with my name, then turned back to look for the next student that they were there to collect.

More and more new students joined our group. When all the names were matched up with the newcomers, we had grown into an impressive small crowd. Grouped into teams of three or four people each, we followed one another into a building full of cars – a building just for cars. Wow. My eyes grew bigger despite how exhausted I was.

We piled into several cars, and made a quick stop at the New York Chinatown first for some late dinner. Then our convoy continued on west. About half an hour later, we arrived at the campus of a university in New Jersey. In front of us were a row of low buildings, not at all like the five- or six-story dorm buildings that I was used to in China.

"Why don't you stay in that room?" Once we were inside the large apartment, someone showed me the way to "my room," so I could get ready for bed. And I was truly impressed again.

I had never had my own private room before. Not to mention the elegant park-like setting outside and the spacious living room in the apartment.

"Wow, this is nice. I like America." I thought.

I woke up late Sunday morning, refreshed. The air was clean, crisp, mixed with an unfamiliar smell of cut grass and fragrant flowers. The sky was a beautiful hue of deep blue. And there was no fog, not even a cloud, in the sky. In front of the dorm building, there was a large span of beautiful green lawns. I was awed, fascinated, and so very delighted.

After lunch, one of the hosts advised me, "You can make a call to tell your parents that you have arrived safely. Just don't talk too long. International calls are expensive, and calculated by the minute."

Really? I could call home? Wow, these students were so kind, and thoughtful. Though mostly strangers, they came all the way out to pick us up from LaGuardia Airport. They drove us in their own cars to this nice school in New Jersey. They fed us. They let me stay in such a nice room by myself, and told me to make an expensive call to my parents.

I got the dialing instructions and called home.

On the third ring, Mom picked up. She sounded like she just woke up from her sleep. Once she realized it was from me though, she became fully alert. She was very happy and relieved that I got there safely and that I called. I quickly told her that everything went smoothly. Flying was cool and everything was perfect. That I had my own private room at the moment. But I was not sure when I would be going to New York City and what was going to happen there. Though I was sure that it would be just as wonderful as well. I promised her that I would write more details in my letter. Quickly said goodbye, I hung up the phone before hitting the one-minute mark.

That afternoon, the friend that Wendy sent to pick me up from the airport, John, found me. He pulled me aside, and introduced himself. Then he handed me a check for a thousand dollars from Wendy, and told me that Wendy thought I would probably need it.

I was astounded. I had never seen a personal check before. And why would I need so much money? My four hundred dollars was still safe and sound in my pocket. But I took the check and put it into my wallet carefully. It was amazing to see a small piece of colorful paper with a few words on it could represent a thousand dollars. Wendy hadn't mentioned anything about lending me money, or that I would need more of it.

Even though I did not know it at the time, Wendy realized just how ill-prepared I was for this trip from our short conversation a few days earlier.

And she was absolutely right.

John asked if I had secured a place to stay in New York City. I told him that I had not and that I would think the school had something arranged for me. He was quiet for a few minutes. Then he suggested that we leave early next morning, to go to the school, and see what they might be able to do for me there.

CHAPTER SIX

THAT NIGHT, I DIDN'T JOIN THE OTHERS WATCHING TV IN the living room. Instead, I went back to "my room" to re-pack my suitcases. I felt that I needed to take care of these beloved creatures of mine, my faithful and only companion from home.

I closed the door, laid the suitcases down on the floor, and opened them. I took everything out. Then I followed Dad's method: folded the clothes, blanket and sheets, carefully and nicely; wrapped the knife; stuffed the soapbox; and put both of my cooking pots back to where they belonged.

And then, gently but firmly, I used my knees to push down on the covers to close them properly. Everything went back inside as it should be, nice and neat. Dad would be proud that I learned well, I thought happily. I stood the luggage up and moved them to the side of the room. Unlike the luggage that I had used when I went to college, these large suitcases were fancy. They had two tiny wheels at one end of the bottom. We could tilt them up from the other side and pull them. So it was much easier to move them around than the ones that we used in college, which had no wheels and had to be lifted up by the straps that we tied on them.

The next morning, John and I thanked our hosts and bid our goodbyes. We each picked up one of the large suitcases. John also carried the small suitcase. And I had my red shoulder bag, now closed tight to safeguard my important documents inside.

Keeping my large suitcase balanced while pulling it on the uneven ground was actually a lot harder than I thought. Our fifteen-minute trip to the bus station was a struggle, as we tried to keep the suitcases upright while they tilted one way or another, on the pebble-covered long path.

The bus took us halfway to New York City. We were to take the subway for the rest of the way to Manhattan, John explained.

Wait, what?

Subway? *The* New York City subway? Nobody had said that I would need to take the subway. Wasn't it super dangerous? Weren't people killed all the time on the New York subway? Like in the movies that I had seen. Even though maybe I had only seen a couple of movies about New York City, but wasn't that enough already?

"Yes, we will take the subway. It's okay." John reassured me like it was not a big deal. How could he be so casual about such a dangerous place? But I closed my mouth as I guessed that he was risking his own life too. So, what more could I say?

At least there was an escalator to get us down to the platform, which helped tremendously with our heavy luggage. Once on the subway, we were able to tuck my large suitcases away into a corner and sat down on the shining plastic bench ourselves. John put my small suitcase by his feet while I held my red bag tightly on my lap.

"It will take about an hour to get to downtown Manhattan. Just relax." John told me, as he leaned back to read some newspaper that someone left on the seat next to his.

Relax? I wasn't sure how I could. I looked around nervously.

This was close to the middle of the day. The subway car was not very crowded, with about half of the seats empty. Most people there were just minding their own business. A few passengers were reading newspaper or books. A girl looked to be in her early 20s, who seemed to be a student, was writing on her notebook. She crouched over her knee, not at all concerned about her safety or what was going on around her. A few people were talking with their companions. A young mom was holding on to the handle of a stroller, talking to her baby inside and making him giggle. Quite a few of the passengers had their eyes closed, and some of them, including one who looked like a homeless person, were clearly asleep.

Hmmm, if people acted like this, maybe the New York City subway was not as dangerous as in those movies, I thought. I looked around and registered my two large suitcases in the corner, my small case at John's feet, and squeezed my red bag on my lap slightly.

"Okay, all four pieces are still here." I sighed, finally feeling a little bit relaxed myself.

Our ride was uneventful. Pretty soon, we were back up onto the ground, seeing sunlight again. But the scenery had changed. There were many more cars rushing around on the much narrower streets. Nearly half of them were those famous New York City yellow taxi cabs. The air reeked with the smell of exhaust from the vehicles. The sky was grey. Filtered sunlight cast long shadows by the buildings along the streets.

Most of the buildings were tall. Some of them were so tall that the top parts of which seemed to have disappeared into the clouds.

"They must be those so-called 'skyscrapers' like in the movies." I thought.

Much more majestic and powerful in real life, the buildings seemed to be oozing with stories and history. They lined the streets, jagged in their heights, texture, and colors, like an army in formation though with mismatched uniforms. Many seemed to be built with huge rocks, with graceful statues carved into the design.

And they must have been standing there for decades, if not over a century, watching the world go by, watching people like us. They appeared to be suspicious of newcomers like myself.

"Who are you and what are you going to do here?" they seemed to be asking me. "Are we going to like you?"

I tried to ignore them and their questions, and looked on.

There were a few small parks here and there, decorated the city-scape. Resident kids were having fun in the playground, running, sliding, and laughing. A little kid was chasing pigeons on the sidewalk in front of us. His mom walking behind him with her hands full of bulging shopping bags.

The sky was cloudy here in Manhattan. It was a calm day and the street was fairly quiet. We dragged the heavy suitcases along the street, around some very large buildings. And we still had all my four pieces of luggage as I counted them again.

Just as I started to wonder how much further we would need to go, John signaled for us to turn into an ordinary looking brick building. The old metal cage elevator was really crammed when we got the suitcases and ourselves into it.

"We will leave your luggage at my place first." John explained.

He was probably an engineering student, I guessed. Because of my parents' professions, I grew up with a lot of engineers. Most of them were very smart but quiet, not unlike John. John wore glasses, had few words to say, though almost everything he said was right on point and necessary. His apartment was equally crammed, a big contrast to the dorm in the countryside of New Jersey from last weekend. I guessed I should have expected such as we were now in Manhattan, crowded like in Beijing.

John's bedroom was very small. He had no bed frame. A few mattresses piled on top of one another, mismatched in size and colors, was his bed. I was not sure why he had so many mattresses. Maybe it was to gain a little height so he didn't have to feel like he was sleeping on the ground?

At the foot of his bed there was a gap just wide enough to slide my large suitcases in between the mattresses and the wall. So there they went. Then we put my small suitcase on top of the large ones. And I kept my red bag on me with all my important items inside.

The other half of John's room housed a small table and a chair. With the two of us standing there, the room felt jammed. I found myself breathing easier again when we left his room after putting the suitcases away.

Outside of his bedroom was a small hallway, with a door that led to a tiny bathroom, and a small area served as a kitchen. Across the hallway was a second bedroom. John told me that was for his roommate, another NYU student who came from Europe.

They had a small dining table that leaned onto the hallway wall, with half of its surface taken by bottles of condiments. A steel sink was set in between a two-burner stovetop and a beat-up refrigerator. Hmmm, everything was packed together. Not much unlike our apartment home in Beijing, except his apartment was even smaller, and really dim with just a small window at the far end of the kitchenette.

"Do you want to eat anything?" John asked.

"No. Let's just go to the school." I answered.

I was not hungry, though quite anxious to find out what kind of place I would be able to call home from now on. John led the way out of his apartment and locked the door behind us. Once again, we walked onto the street of this world-famous city. This was a strange land for me, but it was to become my new home from now on.

And I held my curiosity back, as my concern continued to grow about where I would be able to stay for the night.

"School is mostly closed for the summer break," John explained, "but I think the student services office might be open."

I didn't know how to respond to that.

"Someone has to be here, right? They asked me to come in mid-August. And now I am here. They need to tell me what to do and where to go. And most importantly, I need them to tell me where I can live from now on." I kept these thoughts to myself, couldn't wait to get the answers from the school officials.

The office we went to was quite large. Though like everywhere else we had been today, not very crowded. We waited in a short line. A middle-aged lady came over to talk to us when it was my turn.

I knew she was speaking perfect American English, but I had *no idea* what she was saying, not at all. I just stared at her. Sounds were coming out of her mouth, fast and furious. Though they were nothing but an absolutely unintelligible gabble to me. I looked to John in a panic for his help, as I was completely lost. John realized my challenge and started to talk to the lady on my behalf.

I didn't know what they were saying, but I could tell there was no good news that I was hoping for. Here and there, I caught a word or two, ".... she.... we.... don't.... school.... back.... you.... closed.... back.... can't.... tell her.... Nothing.... No.... I don't...."

Though each time she turned to me to explain, my brain would turn into mush. And I would not understand a single word from her. But when she talked to John, I would grasp a word or two every few seconds.

John translated for me, "She said that the school is closed for the summer break right now, so they don't have anything for you. But if you want to apply for the dorm for the fall semester, it's $570 a month to share a studio with a roommate."

"Wait. Slow down." my brain screamed.

What was a "studio?" Five hundred and seventy dollars a month? That was about half of what my parents had saved after 30 years, for one month? Every month? And that was shared with someone else still?

The lady brought over a brochure with a picture of a floor plan that she opened up to show me and explained.

"A studio," she pointed, "is one room that has everything inside. You sleep on the bed here. Your roommate sleeps on the other bed across from yours. You eat at the table there. The stove is here. And the bathroom is here..."

Hmmm, stove *and* bathroom inside, I had never seen anything like it. But it made sense to cram everything into one small space. Now that I started to get a taste of the tight space and sky-high expenses here in Manhattan.

And no, I didn't want to spend that much money just for a place to live.

"Any other options?" I asked John. He translated.

The lady shook her head. "No, this is the only option that our school offers. And it's not available until the middle of September. If you need something now, you will have to go find it on your own." she advised.

On my own? When? Where? How?

I had so many questions that my head started to spin. And I needed a place to stay for tonight. Where was I going to go tonight?

My panic returned. My heart was racing again. The lady sensed my anxiety and became quite sympathetic.

"You should go home and come back in a month." she suggested.

"Go home? Are you kidding me? Go home? Back to Beijing?" I screamed in my head. "Does she have *any* idea about the hell that I have gone through? And put my whole family and so many others through, just so I can be here today? Because the school, *your* school, has asked me to come a month early?"

This was not at all what I had expected.

But what did I expect?

That blank, mysterious world behind the fog?

Frankly, the only story I vaguely remembered hearing on the reception received from a US school, was from one of my close friends at USTC, Stacy. Like Faye, Stacy's boyfriend, Jonathan, another super intelligent guy from our class, had graduated and come to the US a year earlier. He told Stacy in a letter that the school had everything ready for him when he arrived: a guest apartment for him to stay in, an agenda on what he needed to do, where to go for sightseeing or shopping, and more.

They also introduced him to other students and staff. Jonathan was very pleased and impressed in his report, as Stacy shared with us. Sure he went to Harvard. But an American university was an American university, right? Why should I expect NYU to be any different?

In fact, at that moment, I realized that I had never even thought of any other possibilities. I just assumed that if I showed up at NYU, they would have all the arrangements for me. Just like when I entered my middle school, high school, and college, where the only decision that I needed to make was to choose which bunk bed I wanted to sleep in.

John was trying still. But the lady was only shaking her head now. No, nothing she could do. "School is closed for the summer and will remain closed until fall semester starts again in a month. The dorm is also closed..."

"Wait," I perked up, "if the dorm is closed, there is nobody living in there, right? Can't they just let me live there for the next month? If I have to pay $570 for a month and share it with a stranger, so be it. I would take it."

And with that thousand dollars that Wendy lent me, I could afford a month's rent in the dorm. I needed a place to stay. Where was I going to stay, like for *tonight*? I asked John to translate that question for me.

"Oh no. No, no. You can't. It's closed. I am sorry. Go home and come back in a month." The lady's voice started to take on a distraught edge.

After another 30 minutes of such back and forth, I realized that this was a brick wall that I kept hitting my head against. And I was not going to break it. It was not going to help me to get anywhere by trying to negotiate with this lady any more. She obviously had done everything she could think of by this point. I looked at John, and it was the same answer. He had already exhausted what he could say also. He had dutifully translated everything. There was obviously nothing more that he could do either.

I took the application form for the school dorm and stopped my fight. It was five hundred and seventy dollars a month and I had to wait a whole month to get in? But what other alternatives did I have?

By the time we left NYU, it was already late in the afternoon. John asked if I was hungry. And I realized that my stomach was a hard knot again. No, I didn't need to eat anything, I needed to find a place to sleep tonight.

Still, John bought something from a street vendor and got me something too. He finished his quickly. I thanked him, and swallowed mine fast without paying much attention to the food. I was still preoccupied by the thought of not having a place to stay for the night.

"What should I do?" I asked John.

"Maybe find a place yourself." he answered simply. "Five hundred and seventy dollars a month is a lot." he added.

That, surprisingly, gave me some comfort. "Oh good, so I don't have to stay in the school dorm. And there is hope that I won't have to spend that much money just for a place to stay either. But how can I find a place on my own, and do that quickly?"

In this new country and this scary city, where I didn't know anyone and not able to communicate with anyone (other than John, but obviously he didn't have any other recommendation either), how could I find a home quickly?

Soon it was completely dark outside. We still had not come up with a good plan. And I couldn't delay going back to John's cramped apartment anymore. Though once we got back to his room, as I looked around, I simply could not see a solution there either. There just wasn't enough space in that cramped unit that I could fit.

"Where will I be sleeping tonight?" The question echoed in my head. It bounced around endlessly. But I dared not to ask John, afraid to hear what his answer might be.

Now, don't get me wrong. John seemed to be a very nice guy. A perfect gentleman. He had helped me, a complete stranger, tremendously in the last couple of days. But he was a guy and a complete stranger to me. Just because Wendy knew him didn't mean that I knew him enough to feel at ease like an old friend. Not to mention to sleep in the same room with a guy? Any guy? And where in that room would there be a space for me to sleep?

"Dad will kill me (actually more like he would take me back home in a heartbeat) if he knew that may be what I will have to do tonight."

Other than my family, I had *never* slept in the same room with a guy, not even with Connor. But there was no indication of any other possibility or arrangement for the night, on this island called Manhattan.

"Do you want to call Wendy?" John asked, pulling me back from my thoughts.

"Yes. That would be great." I felt a slight hope. Maybe she would have some ideas.

"Okay, here's the phone. I will go take a shower first." John left the room, closed the door behind him.

I called Wendy, thanked her for finding John to get me from the airport, and that I was grateful for all the help he had provided. I also told her that I was surprised and appreciated her foresight in lending me the thousand dollars. Now I realized that I very likely would indeed need it. Then, I unloaded my big concern.

"I don't know what the plan is for tonight," I told her, "I mean his room is small. And I don't know where I would sleep."

Wendy responded lightly, "Oh, just kick him out."

Kick him out? What kind of plan was that?

This was his apartment. He lived here. And he had not volunteered to go anywhere else.

In fact, at this very moment, he was on the other side of the wall, taking his shower, getting ready to sleep. I realized that I was on my own at this point, and I had no idea what to do, or what to say. The water in the shower stopped. So I said goodbye to Wendy and waited nervously for John's return.

John came back with a towel on his shoulder, and he was drying his short black hair with it. He looked at me, "Oh, you are done with the call? Why don't you go take a shower too?"

"Sure." I didn't think he was asking.

"Ummm." I hesitated, "Where do you think I could sleep tonight?" I had to ask that question at some point, so it might as well be now.

I did not know if I had imagined it, but I thought his face flushed in the dim light. There was an awkward pause in that tiny room.

"You can sleep on one of these mattresses," he pointed to his pile of mattresses, and said, "I will pull it out."

I didn't know what to say, what to think, or what else to do. Silently, I picked out a set of clean clothes. Not pajamas, but long jeans, a button-up shirt with a long sleeve, and a change of underwear. I left his bedroom and got in the tiny bathroom to shower.

I racked my brain while standing under the water. "John is *the only person* I know in the entire New York City. Unless I count that lady from the school office. What else can I do? Where else can I go? What other options do I have? I can't crack open a door to sneak into one of those empty dorm rooms at the school, as I have no idea where to even find them and how to get in."

But just knowing that there were these empty dorm rooms somewhere on this island made me feel like I should try to do just that. So I didn't have to be at this place, with a stranger, a guy, and spend the night in that tiny room with him.

And I couldn't do what Wendy had suggested, to ask John to leave his own home just so I could sleep better.

I was completely out of ideas. But I couldn't stay in the shower forever either. Turned the water off, I dried myself slowly. Then I put on my clothes, and stepped out of the bathroom.

As I tried to open the door to John's bedroom, I noticed that the door was now blocked from inside and could only open slightly. Squeezed through the crack, I saw one of the mattresses from his pile was now laid out where the empty space used to be, next to the original pile of mattresses. John was sitting on his bed, which had sunken significantly closer to the ground. Obviously, this newly laid out mattress was my bed for the night.

Nothing more to be said. I sat down on the mattress on the floor. John turned off the light, said good night, and laid down on his bed. I smoothed out the sheet of cloth on the mattress, put the shirt that I had just changed out of over the small pillow John gave me, and laid down myself on my "new" bed.

I was tense, rigid as a log of wood. That pair of stiff high-waist jeans I picked out was a bad choice, as its material was so thick that I could feel it cutting into my flesh when I tried to bend my knees.

So I just laid there, straight on my back, looking up into the ceiling. I was super nervous, stressed out, and locked in that position, mentally and physically. I could hear the blood whooshing in my ears, as I listened, to any sound or movement in the room. There were cockroaches in the apartment, and I could hear them scuttling around.

"Hopefully, they won't come onto my mattress or onto me during the night." I pleaded to the universe in my head.

But much more so, I listened to any sound from the mattress butted against mine. Oh, I knew that if my friend Wendy trusted John, I should too. And he had been nothing but nice, respectful and helpful. But I just was never in such a situation like this before, ever. Daddy had always drilled in me that whenever I was alone in a room with a guy, I needed to keep the door open as wide as possible. And always try to do whatever I could to avoid putting myself in such a situation to begin with.

I couldn't sleep. I didn't know if it was the jetlag, the lumpy mattress, or just the amount of stress I was under. In fact, I didn't even notice if the mattress was uneven at all. But it certainly wasn't comfortable.

I just listened, intensely listened. And I could tell that John was not asleep either, for a very long time. We did not talk. I didn't know what he was thinking, or if he also felt awkward. Maybe he should have tried harder, to ask a friend or something, to find a place for me to stay with a girl, or for him to go stay with a guy friend somewhere.

I listened to the cockroaches. I listened to the soft ticking of the second hand of my watch, still on my left wrist. My left hand was placed on top of my right hand, both folded over on my belly.

It seemed to me that when people were dead, they would often be positioned like this. Laying on their backs, straight and rigid like a log, with their hands folded on top of one another, over their bellies. I didn't know why I was even thinking about dead people (even though I had never even seen one in real life). Or why it seemed to be the case how they were laid. But it was an image that persisted in my head throughout that night.

Tick, tick, tick... Scuttle, scuttle, scuttle...

I didn't know how long it had passed. Or what time it was. But eventually I heard the even breathing sound coming from John. Knowing that he was finally asleep seemed to help me to relax a little. Still, it took me a very long time, even after that, to doze off for a little bit, just before the room started to light up from the morning sun.

CHAPTER SEVEN

Breakfast was some simple toast. I finished my piece fast, couldn't wait to get out of this small apartment. Somehow, even though I had no idea on exactly how, I decided at that moment that I would find another place to stay, and would *not* be back to John's room for another night.

As I insisted, John and I went back to the university office where we found the same lady from yesterday. I tried again to convince her to let me move into the dorm now.

"The dorm is empty, not used, not making money for the University. Please let me stay there. Please!" I pleaded.

"I will pay! Five hundred and seventy dollars or whatever."

"I will sign the lease... If I have to stay there for the entire school year, I will. Please just let me in. I need it today."

With John's help and my broken English, I asked. And I tried different angles to build myself a stronger case. But no matter how I bargained, she insisted just as firmly that it was not possible.

"It is closed. There is nothing we can do for you. Please just go home and come back in a month."

Well *that*, was still not an option for me.

John took more pity on me and started to rack his brain harder, tried to figure something else out. "Hey, there is another alumnus from USTC at NYU." he remembered.

"Do you know Martin?" John asked. "He was from your college as well."

"No, I don't." I told him truthfully.

But I was eager to take any help I could get. So I asked for Martin's contact information. John pulled out a little address book from his pocket, found Martin's office phone number in there, and gave it to me.

I called Martin right away from the Student Services office. The lady gladly provided a phone for me to use, and wished me luck in finding a solution that their office could not provide at the moment.

"Sure. Come on over." Martin said over the phone.

He told me the building name and room number for his office. I headed over by myself, releasing John from my troubles. So he could catch up on all the things he hadn't been able to take care of for himself over the last couple of days.

Martin had a desk in a very large office, inside the Physics Department. The office was empty except for him. Martin explained that it was always quiet during the summer break because most people were on vacation. I told him that I needed to find a place to stay and asked for his advice.

He thought for a second and instructed me. "Around the corner of this building is Broadway. Take a right there and head downtown to Chinatown. Find a newspaper booth. Buy today's 星岛日报 (Sing Tao Daily newspaper). Then you can come back here to call the rental places."

Wait, what?

Did he say that I needed to go to Chinatown? *The* Chinatown in New York City? The Chinatown where people got murdered just like in the New York City subway? Wasn't it super dangerous? And he was sending me there *by myself*?

And Broadway? Wasn't that the world famous street for all the acting and theaters? We were next to *that* Broadway?

My head was spinning. And my anxiety had flared up again.

"Can you take me there?" I pleaded, finding myself in that uncomfortable and helpless position several times since I got here in Manhattan.

"Oh, no. No need. It's right there. Super easy to find. You can bring back the paper and make calls here." he said lightly. Pointing at the empty desk next to his, Martin pushed the black corded rotary telephone set toward it.

"You will see. It's easy to find." he reassured me again, and went back to reading his thick textbook.

I rose slowly, hesitating. I wanted to ask him one more time but realized that it would not make any difference. Both John and Martin were doing their best already to help me, someone who they had just met. And the rest was on me. I just needed to get on with it and get it done.

And who knows, maybe Chinatown would be fine just like the subway.

Reluctantly I walked out of Martin's office. I took an elevator downstairs, and got out of the building. "Wow. Fancy elevators they have here." I observed, couldn't remember if I had seen such nice elevators in any building back in China.

Once outside the building, I looked around, not sure which direction I should go. Somehow, my instinct told me that I needed to act as if I knew where I was going. And I shouldn't behave like a new girl from China, who was completely lost and thoroughly scared. Even though it was only my second day in this city. Even if I *was* lost. Even if I *was* terrified. And I still did not understand most of the words people had said. I had to act differently. I had to act with confidence, regardless of how I felt.

I remembered Martin had said to find Broadway first, so I walked to the corner of the street. Right there, hanging on the light post across the intersection, was a green street sign with white letters "Broadway" on it.

My heart skipped a beat, "Yes! Small victories!"

I took a deep breath and turned right onto that world-famous street. "Wow, if I have told Mom and Dad that I am walking on *the* Broadway by myself, they will be so proud. And maybe a little concerned too."

I kept on walking and scanning for more street signs. "Fourth Street," "Third Street." Okay, the numbers were getting smaller like Martin had said that they should. So I was headed in the right direction toward Chinatown.

The street names were words now, instead of numbers. And more and more store signs along the street were in Chinese. Though they were in a very different style than what I was used to seeing in China.

I tried to walk as if I had been on this street thousands of times, though in my mind, the lingering question for what I was searching for was still a very basic one, "What does a newspaper booth look like?"

The answer came not too much later. Up ahead about half a block away at the next intersection, there was a round green structure on the sidewalk, with the side facing me wide open. Lots of newspapers and magazines lined the sides of the stand.

I walked closer and saw that most of these publications were actually printed in Chinese. And right there, slightly off the center on the ground, was a tall stack of newspaper with the one on top in big black-and-red ink, printed Sing Tao Daily in Chinese.

"Yeah! I found it! This is terrific!"

I waited till it was my turn and told the guy inside the booth: "I will have a Sing Tao Daily." in Mandarin.

He looked at me strangely. As if he could tell that it was my first solo-trip in this city and to Chinatown. Then, he stretched his hand out toward me. Ummm, wasn't he supposed to give me the newspaper? I looked at him, baffled.

He got a little impatient, "Money." he barked, with a strong Cantonese accent.

"Oh, yes." I swung my red bag to the front of me, opened it. I found my wallet inside, and took out a green dollar bill quickly and handed it over to him.

He took the money but still didn't give me any paper. There were some rustling sounds and clicking of coins. Then he extended out his arm again, holding something in his loose fist. I put my hand out, and he dropped some coins into my palm.

"How about the newspaper?"

I asked tentatively, not certain at all what the proper way was to buy a newspaper here in America. Even though it was in Chinatown. Even though I was buying a Chinese newspaper. Everything still felt completely foreign to me.

"Just take one." he said offhandedly. With his head bent down, he seemed to be done with me already.

I kneeled down, and tried to pick up the paper. But I was surprised to see that it was wrapped into a big stack of papers.

"What is this? Why do they fold so many pages all into one bundle?" I thought in my head, puzzled. The newspaper in China was simply one large printed page folded over itself a couple of times.

"Take the bundle." the guy from inside the booth barked again.

"This whole thing?" I was really confused. This was a *daily* newspaper? Why so much? But I was not here to argue with him or to show him how little I knew about things here in the US, and that I was so confused about everything. So, I took one large bundle of the paper, stood up, and turned back toward the way where I came from.

Not even fifteen steps out, I was startled by this black guy who jumped right in front of me. He blocked my way, and forced me to stop on my tracks. He was talking loud and fast, to *me*. And he was waving his arms around like he was trying to tell me something. But I had no idea what he was saying. Did I do something wrong? Was he trying to rob me? I looked at his unkempt face, his long and messy hair, his old and dirty clothes, and took notice of an unpleasant smell from him. He must be one of those homeless people here.

"And what does he want? Why is he talking to me? What is he saying? Why is he talking louder now, and faster? Why is he getting upset with me? What did I do?"

All these questions were racing in my head, but I had no answer to any of them. My confusion must be quite obvious now, as he started to add even more gestures, waving his arms even more wildly around. And he kept pointing backwards in the direction of the newspaper booth.

I still could not understand a single word that he was saying. But my gut told me to look back. So I did. The guy inside the newspaper booth was calling me from where he was sitting and gesturing for me to go back.

"I must have taken way too much newspaper."

I thought in dismay and felt embarrassed. Blood rushed into my face. I turned and walked back quickly. I tried to look into the stack that I took, to see if there was another cover page to indicate a second or even more sets of the paper in the bundle, but somehow I didn't find any.

When I got back to the booth, I saw something in the hand that the clerk had thrust forward toward me. It was some paper. Some green paper. It was money. He shoved the money toward me and told me to take it. So I did. Then he stopped yelling and went back to tend his own business. I looked at the bills he gave me. There were a few different ones, though all green in color. I looked at him uncertainly, still confused. He looked up and saw my face.

"You gave me a twenty." he seemed to be getting mad again, and upset that I was so slow and causing him all this trouble.

And finally it dawned on me that he and the homeless guy took the time and effort to get me back here, not because I took too much of the newspaper, but because he wanted to give me the rest of my change. Since I gave him a $20 bill instead of a $1 bill as I thought. My heart suddenly felt warm and my eyes got misty. I quickly thanked him. Put the money carefully back into my wallet, I turned and walked away again.

I walked slower this time with that same stack of newspaper tucked back under my arm.

"How could I be so careless," I berated myself, "almost lost $19. At this rate, I would run out of money really fast!"

I just learned another lesson. To be more careful with money here. Since unlike Chinese RMB, the USD bills looked the same – same size and same color – regardless of their denominations.

But what jolted me even more was the honesty from the newspaper-booth clerk. Even though I was sure he wouldn't mind to have some extra cash. He chose to do the right thing to correct a mistake that *I* had made. Even the homeless person had gone out of his way to make sure that I, a complete stranger, was not short-changed. Their actions and kindness moved me in a profound way that was completely unexpected. Especially from this new scary city called New York.

When I passed the same black guy again, I noticed that he was watching me from his spot at the foot of the building now, calm and silent. He was no longer talking or waving of his arms. He just sat there quietly, leaned back onto the wall, and observed the world in front of him. I looked him in the eyes, thanked him, and walked on by.

BACK AT THE office at NYU Physics Department, Martin pointed out the classified section that listed available rental places on the newspaper to me. He advised me to mark out the ones that fall in my price range. Then I shall call them for details and book viewing appointments before I go see these places in person. He also suggested that I started my search in Chinatown. For its close proximity to the school, and relative ease of communication. I pored over the newspaper and marked out the cheapest room rental places.

Before I made any call though, Martin asked me if I knew Shirley. She was one of the girls from our class. Of course I knew her. Although we weren't roommates or particularly close, there just weren't that many girls in our school. And we had many classes together in the last five years.

"Shirley is in Brooklyn." Martin told me.

"And where is that?" I asked.

"Oh, it's not far. Probably one hour by subway." He wrote down her room and phone number on a small piece of paper and handed it to me.

I was thrilled. Wow, a girl from my class was right here in New York City.

I called Shirley right away. Though an American guy answered the phone. I wasn't certain if I had dialed a wrong number, but asked for her room number as written on Martin's note regardless.

"Hold on," he said. A couple of minutes later, Shirley picked up the phone.

I was overjoyed to hear her voice. I told her that I was in Manhattan and didn't have a place to stay.

"How did you find a place?" I asked her.

"Oh, I am in our school dorm."

How come their school dorm was open? I wondered in my head, and why wasn't NYU's open?

"You can come over if you want," she invited me warmly, "but I have a few roommates."

"Oh, that will be amazing. It's okay, I don't mind having other girls there." I rushed.

All my years living in the dorms in China, we almost always had six girls in the same room. And sometimes we had visitors staying over as well. So, I was used to being in crowded dorm rooms. Shirley gave me the directions to her school. The right subway that would take me there. The name of her stop. And how to find her building after I got off the train.

"It may look a little scary," she added at the end, "but you should be fine."

After hanging up with Shirley, I called John at his office. I told him that I would be staying with someone from my school that night, and that I needed to pick up my small suitcase from his place.

LATER THAT AFTERNOON, with my small suitcase in one hand, and my big red bag slung across my shoulder, I got down onto a subway platform again. This time, I was traveling alone.

Almost everyone else on that train was an African American. Maybe that was why Shirley had said that it could look "a little scary?" I was indeed a little nervous. And I noticed that a few people looked at me as if they were wondering if I was there by mistake, or that they didn't think I belonged there.

But I was not too worried. Especially after my morning encounter with the helpful black homeless guy. Most importantly, I was just really relieved that I would have a place to stay for the night with other girls. And one of them was someone whom I already knew. I was so happy that Martin had told me about Shirley. And that I wouldn't have to go back to John's place for another night.

Though it surprised me to see guys and girls in the same hallway inside Shirley's dorm building, as we always had separate living quarters or even separate dorm buildings in China for boys and girls. Shirley's dorm room itself almost felt familiar. There were several girls in the room and all of them came from China. Bunk beds lined both sides of the walls. There wasn't any extra bed for me to sleep in, as the room was already crowded when I arrived. But Shirley helped me to set up a makeshift bed by pulling a couple of chairs together. Since I was pretty small, it worked out just fine.

The wooden chairs were a bit tough to sleep on. I also had to be careful when turning, so I didn't topple over and fall on my face. But I slept well that night. Not troubled at all by any sound or anything else in the world.

Though despite Shirley's desire in helping me, I realized that her roommates did not share her willingness. By the next afternoon, when I did not leave their campus, I heard impatient tones from some of the girls already. I didn't pay too much attention to it initially. I was still immersed in my enjoyment of feeling safe and relaxed. And reflected on how the first two days in New York City could have felt like an endless of struggle already.

But Shirley's roommates started to make it more obvious that they didn't share my joyous mood. That evening, as I was going back from the washroom, I heard some loud arguments that suddenly stopped as I walked into the room. And I caught some dismayed stares shooting over at Shirley's direction from her roommates. I did not want to pry, though I realized that I couldn't stay there much longer. But I didn't say anything. I just silently tried to keep it to myself and be as little of a burden as possible.

That night, as I tried to pull the same chairs together again to make my "bed," Shirley's roommates started to protest.

"I need my chair," said one girl, shooting another agitated glance at Shirley. I looked back and saw that Shirley was almost in tears. She gave me her own chair and looked at another roommate silently until that girl gave up, and let me took her chair as well.

After the light was turned off, someone in the room muttered "We aren't allowed to let anyone else stay here. You'll get us in trouble." Obviously, that was meant for me and Shirley as if she was making them harbor a fugitive right there in their own dorm room. I felt bad for Shirley, but I did not know what I could do or say, nor did I have any solution to those complaints at that moment. So, I stayed quiet, tried to go to sleep, and decided that I would deal with this in the morning.

The next morning, Shirley asked me if I would be going back to NYU to look for a place to stay. I told her that was indeed my plan. Then I asked her if it would be okay for me to come back and stay with them for one more night, *if* I didn't find anything.

Shirley was silent for a while. I could see her struggle and suspected that her roommates would not let her keep me there anymore. Finally, she led me outside to the end of the hallway and showed me a sofa at a little alcove near the staircase. A couple of guys were sitting there watching a sports program on a TV set hanging on the opposite wall.

"Can you sleep here then?" she pointed at the sofa. She was clearly struggling between her desires to help me and trying to keep peace with her roommates.

I looked at the sofa, the guys sitting there, and all the students passing by that area. Then I looked at Shirley. I didn't say anything, as I didn't know what to say. I knew she was doing everything she could for me. Though in my head, the only answer was a loud and firm "No."

No, I couldn't sleep in a hallway where anyone and everyone could walk by at any time. At that moment, I realized that I also could not come back here tonight and put her in such a tough spot again.

But where could I go?

I didn't know what to say to Shirley. The dorm was not just for her to use. They had rules and other roommates to consider. We went back to her dorm in silence. I retrieved my red canvas bag, and quietly took a few extra changes of clothes and my toothbrush from my small suitcase, and stuffed them into my red bag. I said goodbye to Shirley and left their school.

INSIDE THE SUBWAY train that was heading back to downtown Manhattan, I stood in front of an empty seat and held onto an overhead handle. Swaying with the rhythm of the fast-moving train, I tried to not think or dwell on the feelings of abandonment, sadness and hurt. It felt like I had been dropped from a spoiled and well-pampered-baby status in China, to suddenly an ugly orphan that nobody wanted, here in New York City.

I also felt bad for Shirley for taking the heat from her new roommates, simply because she wanted to help me. But how could they even pressure her to ask me to sleep in the hallway? Would they sleep there themselves? I felt some bitterness in my thoughts and decided that I needed to switch my mind onto something else.

"One step at a time." I told myself. "It's useless to feel sorry for myself. Think. What can I do now? How can I find a place to stay for tonight?"

I remembered Martin's advice and decided that I should stop by Chinatown first, to pick up today's newspaper. Then I could go to Martin's office to look for possible places to rent, and make calls from there to book appointments to see those places.

I needed to find a permanent solution. A suitable place for me to stay for tonight, and all of the future nights.

Chapter Eight

WITH A NEW SET OF NEWSPAPER UNDER MY ARM, AND A folded map tucked inside my red bag, I went back to the office at the Physics Department in NYU. Martin was already there as if he had never left, still working on his thick textbook and writing long equations on scratch papers.

I took up the same spot as I did last time. Laid out the classified section of the newspaper, I pulled the phone over, and started checking and dialing. By the time I marked out six low-cost room rental places that were available and made appointments to go see them, the morning was already over.

I headed out, feeling like a veteran on this Broadway Street, even though it was only my third time there. The rental places that I had planned to see were scattered around, though all in Chinatown, as Martin suggested. They all had low rental costs, which hopefully would provide an answer to my search for a home in this city.

Though my enthusiasm sank significantly when I got close to the first place. Following the map, I went deep inside Chinatown, to the back alleys of the district, and behind some small Chinese restaurants and shops. Buckets of dirty water lined the backdoors of the restaurants, with broken dishes and discarded chopsticks sticking out of the dark liquids. The stench in the air was overpowering in most of these streets. People were moving around, working hard in heavily stained clothes, and stepping into the puddles of dirty water on the street without much care.

Small shipping vans and trucks were double parked on the narrow street, while workers moved baskets of vegetables, meat, and fish. The smells and looks of this scene could ruin most people's appetite. I felt the churn in my stomach and forced my mind to switch to something else, away from the odor and the sight.

"君子远庖厨" ('Gentlemen stay far away from the kitchen'). I was reminded of this old Chinese saying. I always thought it meant that "Gentlemen would stay away from slaughtering animals themselves." Now I realized that there might be other meanings to this proverb. That behind the delicious-tasting and delightful-looking dishes, there could be such nauseating smell and ugliness behind the kitchens. I chuckled silently and shook my head. Somehow the works done by the skillful chefs transformed the dishes and made the food scrumptious. At that moment though, I was not sure if I could stomach any food, no matter how appetizing it might seem.

My steps never slowed as I walked on. Checking the neatly folded map only when I got to some quiet corners of the street, to make sure that I was still headed in the right direction. I bought the map from the same newspaper booth that morning when I got the papers and had strategically folded it small. So it would not be too obvious to others when I had to take a quick glance at it. I didn't want to make it too easy for people to tell that I was a stranger to this area.

And I summoned up a confident look even though I did not feel it. I walked at a rather brisk pace as if I knew exactly where I was headed, and that I belonged there. Even though the entire time I was confused about the street names, questioned myself as to why I was there, and if I could stand to actually live in a place like this. I avoided eye contact with people as much as possible since I was afraid that they could see through this mask that I had put on. I walked on as if I believed that I could find a home in this part of the city. I was willing myself to trust that there might be a miracle that somewhere in this area, there could be a little haven for me to stay from now on.

Westbound

Finally, according to the map, I was supposed to be near the first room rental place. But I couldn't seem to even find the right house number. A row of low-rise old buildings lined the street on both sides. The ground floor looked like the backside of some restaurants and grocery stores, while the second and third floors seemed to be the living quarters for people. The house numbers were hard to find on the worn doors and frames, some may be covered up by posters or cloth that hung over them.

And based on the few places for which I was able to find a street number, the numbering seemed to skip around here and there, making very little sense at all.

A lady who looked to be in her thirties came out of an open door with a bucket of dirty water. She heaved it hard outward, splashing the contents out onto the street. The liquid shined darkly with a layer of oil on top, and the putrid odor from it hung pungent in the air.

I swallowed down the bile that came up to my throat and pushed away my desire to run as far away from this district as possible. I reminded myself that I had no place to stay for tonight and that it would be dark in just a few hours' time. The lady looked up and saw me standing across the narrow street. This was my chance to talk to her, so I rushed over.

"Do you know where I can find house number 38B?" I asked.

"What?" She didn't understand what I had said. I also had a hard time figuring out her short response in Cantonese.

Louder and walked closer, I asked in Mandarin again, "38B." From the few words that I had heard spoken in Chinatown, it seemed that everyone there spoke Cantonese. Cantonese was so different from Mandarin that I could hardly understand any of it at all. Luckily, some of them could speak some Mandarin, even if they had a strong accent. And I certainly hoped that it was the case with this lady as well.

"38B..." she repeated. And this time, she tried Mandarin, "This is 38. B, there is no B..."

I was so relieved to see that she could understand me and spoke some level of Mandarin.

"But the ad says it is 38B." I brought out the newspaper with the ad circled and my notes next to it. 38B, it said right there on the ad.

"38. B..." She was thinking. "B..., is it for rent or are you looking for somebody?" she asked again.

"Rent." I told her.

"I think it's upstairs. The second floor." She pointed. Her gesture really helped with this conversation.

"How do I get up there?" I looked around but couldn't see any staircase.

"Come in here." she beckoned me warmly. And I started to think that maybe with helpful people like her, living in a place like this was tolerable? Maybe I would even get to learn Cantonese too? Especially if it was only three hundred and eighty dollars a month. That was almost two hundred dollars a month less compared to the shared studio dorm at NYU.

I followed her into the dark foyer from where she had just come out. Once my eyes adjusted to the dim light, I could see that the area was also used as a storage room. Our narrow path was lined with liquid-stained cardboard boxes on both sides. We walked through a back door into a small hallway that had two other doors on the sides, and a staircase to the left. Dim daylight filtered in through a small dirty window on top of the staircase, brightened the area slightly, and cast shadows on the broken furniture and boxes littered around.

The lady pointed me in the direction of the staircase before she turned around and went back to her work. I thanked her, then walked up the stairs to the first landing. Upon turning, I found two small children sitting at the top of the second flight of stairs. Dressed in mismatched clothes, they were just as surprised to see me as I was to them.

"Mommy?" The bigger kid of the two, a boy probably around five years of age, called out tentatively. I could hear noises inside. But nobody came out. I waited on the stairs, unable to find a way to pass by these kids in the narrow space.

"MOM!" he called again, louder this time.

"What?!" A lady rushed out. Loud in her Cantonese response to the boy's calling, apparently she was not happy to be interrupted. Seeing me, she bent over and picked up the little girl from the ground, yielding a space just wide enough for me to get through. She looked at me up and down and asked, in heavily accented Mandarin this time,

"You come to see the rental room?"

I nodded. She must be the lady whom I talked to that morning on the phone.

"OK. This way." She turned and led the way.

The little boy jumped up and raced ahead of his mother, excited. I was not a "kid person," had never cared for little kids. And I wasn't sure how I might like it living there with these two little ones in the same unit.

"This room." The lady tilted her head and turned right into a doorway. I followed her.

I didn't know how it was possible, but the room seemed to be half the size of John's room. There was a very small bed inside, maybe a bed for the boy. And it took up pretty much all of the space in that room. A small gap was left between the bed and the other wall, not wide enough to slide in my suitcases even if they were standing on their sides. At the foot of the bed, there was a tiny nightstand that filled up the length of the room.

I couldn't see how my suitcases and I could fit in there at the same time. Either they or I would need to take that bed, but definitely not enough room for both.

So, it took me about an hour to find this place, and about all of five seconds to see everything inside and to kill the idea of possibly living there.

"And the rent is three hundred eighty dollars a month?" I didn't know why I still bothered to ask.

"Yes," she looked at me, "and you pay for half of the utilities."

Utilities? Like for water and electricity? I looked up from the bed. There was one yellow bare light bulb hanging overhead from the middle of the ceiling.

I imagined that a prison cell probably looked like this, but bigger?

"You can cook in the kitchen," she added, "and use the telephone downstairs."

"So how much is the total cost?" I needed to know.

"Maybe four hundred. Or four twenty-five?" she estimated.

I made a mental note to scratch this one off from my list. "The room is way too small, and not all that cheap either. Well, I still have five more places to check out before nighttime," I thought, "this one is not going to work."

Though somehow I decided to not tell the lady that I wouldn't be coming back. I just thanked her, and confirmed her phone number, just in case if I had no other options and somehow changed my mind at the end. And I left.

The next place was not much better.

If I thought by spending enough time there in Chinatown, I could get used to the rancid smell, and wouldn't want to gag so much. I was wrong. As I still had to hold my breath when I walked into the third place.

Later that afternoon, I found myself near the end of the land, facing a large body of water. I was not sure which river, lake, or sea it might be. And no matter how many times I turned around, at that end of the Canal Street, I could not find the number of the house on the little side street where it was supposed to be. This was rental place number 5 on my list. Even though nobody answered the door for number 4, I was pretty sure it was just as un-livable as the first three.

And now, "Where is this place? Does it even exist?" I wondered.

I had already walked around that couple of blocks area more than twice. And if I kept going in the direction that I believed the street numbers were indicating, I would be walking into that water very soon. There wasn't as many people around this neighborhood, except for one creepy guy who planted himself at the corner of the street. And his eyes followed me each time when I passed him by.

"Where is it? And where am I? Am I lost?" I paused for a few seconds to check on my map again, in a spot where the view of the eerie guy was blocked.

At this point, I had to finally concede to myself that I was lost, utterly and completely lost. But I couldn't afford to look like I was lost. I didn't want to act like I was lost. A confident image was still my best weapon. Even if it was just to make myself feel somewhat in control and not let panic take over my heart and my soul.

"Oh, forget it!"

I gave up on the futile hunt for this place and didn't want to walk by that creepy guy one more time. The rental room probably would be just as disappointing as all the previous ones anyways. And this neighborhood made me feel unsettling somehow as well.

The sun was hanging low now over a long bridge leaving Manhattan, to New Jersey maybe. It wouldn't be long before nightfall. And I still had no idea where I could go and stay for tonight. Though in that red bag that I carried around all day, I had everything I needed to settle down for a few nights. Once I found a place to stay. *If* I found a place to stay.

I decided to stop my search for this place and go to the next one – the last one on my list. I had planned this last stop to be in between the far-end of Chinatown and NYU, as I needed to head back up to the school anyways.

As I walked, I realized that I was getting quite tired and hungry, and that it was about time for dinner already. The scenery around the area had shifted. The sidewalk was filled with people now. Some were rushing home in determined steps, while others were picking up vegetables, seafood, and meat on their way for dinner.

Delicious cooking smells permeated the air, while welcoming lights were coming on at the front of the restaurants. Though somehow, I still had no appetite for food even though I had been around restaurants all afternoon. The piece of bread that I bought when I first arrived at Chinatown was long gone. And I had no desire to eat anything else since then.

Somehow I found this last rental place without too much trouble. I wasn't sure if it was an easier target, or that I had gotten better by this time. Regardless, I was very glad to see the light was on inside the unit.

This was it.

The last place for which I had an appointment today. My last hope, and my only hope. As none of the previous places I had seen so far would work, at all.

Someone answered from inside after I knocked a few times on the door. The guy who opened the door looked older than me, but probably not by too many years. Wearing a dirty white T-shirt, he smelled like fish. And he looked at me with a frown.

"You are late."

His Mandarin was better than others whom I had talked to earlier that afternoon, or maybe I started to get more used to their accents. And he was right. I told him when I called in the morning that I should be there before five o'clock. But everything took a lot longer than expected.

"Yeah, sorry. Can you show me the room for rent?"

I apologized but otherwise ignored his comment. Just let me see the room and tell me the cost, which were all that I needed. By now, I felt like a professional room hunter. No need for any small talk or even learning their names, just get down to business, without wasting any time.

The guy sighed. He turned around and led the way. From the back, his t-shirt was stained even heavier, making it look like a large patch of brown in several different shades. And I didn't know how it was possible, but the fishy smell was even stronger now. In fact, I realized that this whole place smelled like fish, rotten-fish. I tried to suppress my gag and to hold my breath. But I had to let it go, and breathed through my mouth reluctantly. I wished that I had the capacity of a diver's lungs to hold my breath for as long as I needed.

Although it didn't take long to know that this place would not work for me either, regardless of how desperate I was at this point. The room was pretty much the same size as all the other ones that I had seen – tiny. But this place was different in a way that its "door" was simply a hanging sheet of plastic like a shower curtain, discolored and murky from years of use.

"How much is the total rent?"

The question came out like a habit that I couldn't seem to break, since this room definitely would not work as I could hardly breathe in there.

And there was no way I would feel safe or comfortable to live in a place like this, with a door that couldn't be closed, and a guy like the one who was standing there right next to me. But I still asked. As if I had to take something tangible, even if it was just a number, a dollar amount, to tell myself that I had done everything I could. That I had tried my very hardest in finding a suitable place to live.

"Four fifty." he answered, as he looked at me, taking notice of the Chinese style clothes that I was wearing.

"All utilities included?" Why was I still asking?

"Yeah, sure."

He was studying my face now. Or, to be more accurate, my mask of a face. My expression was void of any emotion by this time. Somehow it felt like this was how I had always been: no smiling, no cringing, and no emotion. I just needed the facts – just give me the numbers – facts and numbers were something that I could deal with. And they seemed to be the only thing that I could deal with at this point.

"Okay, I'll call tomorrow if I want to take it."

Again, I had no idea why I needed to say these things that I did not mean to do at all.

THE REST OF my walk back to NYU, in the diminishing daylight, took maybe only twenty minutes. But it felt ghastly in a way. At this point, I should be panicking, I should be super anxious and super worried, as I had not seen a single place in which I was willing to consider sleeping tonight, or any night. And I couldn't go back to Shirley's. I wouldn't go back to John's. I had no place to go. I was truly homeless.

But somehow, I felt exactly like that mask on my face, without feeling any emotion – blank, plain, numb – no feeling at all.

Though by this time, I did not need to pretend I knew where I was going anymore. Walking on the Broadway Street, I knew exactly where I was headed. And that was the only thing I knew.

I went back to the Physics Department in NYU. The timing was good for me as Martin was just getting ready to leave.

"Oh, you are back!" Martin greeted me warmly. He seemed to be a little relieved to see me again.

"Did you find a place?" he searched my face.

To Martin, I must looked different from the morning when I left. But it was hard to decipher why and how I was different. I felt different. Like a piece of me had died in the last few hours. Was it hope? Was it pride? Was it my dignity or humanity? I had no energy to even think about it. Though I felt icy-cold and empty inside.

"No." I answered.

"Are you going back to Shirley's?" he asked.

"No." I simply shook my head, sparing him from all the details.

"Do you have another place to go for tonight?"

"No." My voice was getting lower with each short answer.

"What are you going to do?" he asked while putting his bag down on his desk, and sat back in his chair.

"I don't know." And I didn't know if I still cared at this point.

"Anyone else you know around here?" He seemed to be getting a little more concerned, asking more questions in the last two minutes than he had since I met him a couple of days ago.

"I don't know. I don't think so." My voice trailed off.

Everyone I knew in New York had already exhausted their resources in helping me: John, the lady at the Student Service Center, Shirley, and Martin here. Though somehow I still didn't feel any of those strong emotions I should be feeling. The anxious and desperate emotions that I had felt the entire time in my first two days here on this world-famous island, possibly the wealthiest place on earth. None of that mattered to me though. Because none of that had anything to do with me. It seemed that nothing mattered to me anymore.

Martin sensed my lack of enthusiasm for this conversation and turned to face his closed school bag on his desk. Although I didn't believe he was thinking about his school work anymore. I opened the newspaper on the desk mechanically, turned to the classified page, looking, but not really seeing, anything on that paper.

Martin looked up after a few seconds and pulled the telephone back onto his own desk by its coiled black cord. He picked up the hand piece and started dialing. I guessed that he and John were not the only Chinese here in New York, because he made quite a few calls in Chinese.

On the "Room for Rent" section of the classified page, there were rental places outside of Chinatown. After the last several hours spent there, I felt no desire to ever go back to Chinatown again. Brooklyn might be a little scary but it was not terribly far. An hour's train-ride should be doable for a daily commute.

"That's how long it takes for Mom and Dad to go to their work each way on the shuttle bus from Mom's school. Maybe I should expand out my search to including these areas." I thought.

The sky was completely dark outside of the large windows by now. My stomach started to protest again.

"Tian Li," Martin's voice cut through my thoughts. There was a hint of excitement on his face that I had not seen before.

"Do you know someone named Ray?" he asked.

"Yeah. He was in my class."

I didn't think I had talked to Ray all that much during those years in college though. Ray was a tall and slim guy, always wearing glasses, always smiling. He was super smart like most of our classmates, and quite nice.

"He's at Columbia. You want to check with him?" Martin informed me.

"Sure." What did I have to lose at this point? If nothing came through, maybe I could ask Martin to lock me inside this office when he left for home tonight.

"Hello?" Ray answered the phone on the second ring.

"Hi, Ray. This is Tian Li."

"Oh hey, Tian Li. How are you?" he responded kindly.

"I am good. I am at NYU now. I heard you are also here in New York?" I asked.

"Yeah. I am at Columbia." He seemed to be happy to hear I was also in New York.

"Look," I didn't really know how to say it, and decided that I was just going to get to the point, "I don't have a place to stay…"

Ray cut me off right away. "Oh, come up here. I have a whole guest apartment from the school. There is a sofa in the living room. You can stay here."

Really?! He had a place, and he was offering to let me stay there? He didn't have to worry about any other roommates. And he had a sofa that he was willing to let me sleep in? Ray was someone I knew for years. Someone I had no doubt that I could trust. Even though he was a boy.

"Oh wow. That's great! Are you sure? How do I get there?"

I wrote down the directions. And I looked back at Martin, seeing a big smile on his face. I felt as if a huge rock had just vanished from my stomach.

A few minutes later, I was back on the street, waved goodbye to Martin and thanked him again as we parted our ways. I headed toward the subway station going uptown. Somehow, this area near NYU and the few streets around it started to feel familiar to me already, and no longer so strange or scary. As I walked in determined and vigorous steps, I felt energized and relieved. It was amazing how big of a difference a few minutes could make. And how different I felt now, compared to when I was coming back from Chinatown, completed defeated and drained, less than 20 minutes ago.

About 40 minutes later, I climbed up the stairs of the subway station in the West Harlem area, and looked around in the darkness of the night for Ray.

Almost like Brooklyn, there were mostly African Americans around here. Small groups of youths stood around the subway terminals, smoking, talking, and just plain hanging around. By now, I learned that they were just as friendly and harmless as anyone else, in China, or here in New York City.

From not far, a slim figure was quickly approaching. No longer looked tall compared to many of the Americans here, the figure looked familiar. Ray waved his arm toward me. "Tian Li," he called out. And I walked over quickly to meet him halfway.

"I didn't know which exit you would be coming out of ..." Ray came running, a bit out of breath. "Where's your luggage?" He looked down at my empty hands and behind me.

"Oh. I left them with Shirley and another friend." I told him.

Shirley, Ray and I were at USTC for the past five years together, so Ray knew Shirley as well.

"Oh. Do you need help with your bag?" He really wanted to help.

"I am fine." And I was truly okay, better than he could ever know. We walked together to his guesthouse residence.

"Columbia is really nice. They let us use these apartments." Ray explained on the way. He had been there for a couple of weeks now, and everything was perfect. How blessed was him, I thought, and how fortunate for me that Martin had found him today.

Once we got to the apartment, Ray graciously showed me around.

"Here's the living room. And that's the sofa you can sleep in. Through this door is the bedroom. And in there, that door leads to the bathroom." he explained.

"You can go use the bathroom anytime you need," he said, "so I think it's easier if I slept in the bedroom."

It was clear to me that Ray had already put in some thoughts into making it more convenient and comfortable for me. Inside my chest, it felt like a large ice block started to melt.

"Here," Ray pointed at a little electrical stove on the coffee table. "I am cooking some ramen noodle. Have you had dinner yet?"

I shook my head. For the first time in days, I realized that even my stomach felt different. It no longer felt like a hard rock, but seemed to be an empty pit.

Ray took out another package of ramen, and set it beside the stove. When the first batch was done, he put it in a bowl and handed it over to me to eat first.

The hot and tasty soup warmed me all the way down to the bottom of my stomach instantly.

Chapter Nine

I WENT BACK HOME, BACK IN BEIJING IN MY PARENT'S ROOM. There were quite a few others there too. Like how it always were, with a few of us sitting on my parents' bed, while Daddy sat on the futon sofa across from us.

Everyone was talking excitedly. They asked me what I had seen so far in the US, and in New York City. I had described to them my first days in New Jersey: the beautiful campus, the friendly students who picked us up from the airport, and the spacious apartment for student dorms. Also about Manhattan: the majestic buildings, the busy streets, the yellow cabs, the tiny apartment and rooms, the not-so-dangerous subways and Chinatown, and the beautiful floors and elevators inside the buildings in NYU.

Among all the voices asking questions and talking, I could hear Mom's voice above it all, as she always got when she wanted to be heard. Pretty soon, the others started to talk among themselves. And I found that I was only half listening, and half lost in my own thoughts.

"What a baby!" I castigated myself. "Just because I have a re-entry visa, because that lady at NYU told me to go home a few times, and I just came back home?! How spoiled am I?! Running to Mommy and Daddy when I encounter some little problems in the US? They must be so disappointed at me right now. Even though they are not showing it. Even though they seem to be relieved to have me back home. And they haven't blamed or judged me at all. All that work that we have done, and all that money that we have spent were for nothing?!"

"No! I can't let this be the end! I have to go back to the USA! I have to go back to New York City! I will start school at NYU!"

I was talking myself into a strong commitment for what needed to be done. And I realized that I had broken into a cold sweat, reflecting on how fortunate that I actually could do it, as "it is such a pure serendipity that I got a two-entry visa on my passport. And I thought it would be a waste. But now I actually will need to use it so I can go back to the US again."

"But where will the money come from, to pay for another airline ticket to go back to New York? And how did I even get back here at home in the first place? Where did I get the money to buy the airline ticket for coming back? And where did I leave my luggage?" My thought started to jump around.

At that moment I suddenly realized that the room was quiet and that everyone had stopped talking. They were all looking at me now. They seemed to be concerned somehow. And they were all waiting for me to say something. Maybe they had asked me a question that I did not hear.

I looked at them. Looking into their eyes, I spoke up, slowly, though loudly and clearly, not sure if I was telling them or myself.

"I have a second entry visa. I *will* go back to the USA. I will. I will find a place to stay! I will go back before school starts! And I will go back very soon!"

I spoke with such unwavering certainty and determination. But somehow I realized that tears were roll down my face in streams, no matter how much I hated to let them see me cry.

AND THAT WAS when I always woke up from this dream, on Ray's sofa in his living room, sobbing, in the darkest moment of the night. My face was awash from tears. The light pink t-shirt that I used to cover up the makeshift pillow – the armrest of the couch – was already soaking wet.

That same dream hunted me every single night for the next several nights, in Ray's apartment, in that little safe haven that I had found in New York City.

EVERY EVENING, I pored over the newspaper I purchased earlier that day. I combed through the rental ads and check their locations on the map. And if both location and price looked good, I circled the ad on the paper, and marked the location on the map. I then called the landlord to see if it was still available and booked appointments to go see those place the very next day.

My search area grew bigger each day. It soon covered almost the entire Manhattan, as well as Brooklyn, Queens. And toward the end, I was even ready to consider some closer parts of New Jersey.

Every morning, I headed out of the door, with the map and the classified page of the newspaper stuffed in my red messenger bag. And I took the subway to go check out those places.

For the first couple of days, when I got hungry, I bought some cheap street food for lunch, and gulped them down quickly while I walked from one place to the next. Inevitably my stomach did not like it. And by early afternoon, I had to find a trash can somewhere on the street and threw up into it until my stomach was empty again. Feeling better, I kept going and stayed out till nightfall, until no landlord would see me anymore. Then I went to purchase that day's newspaper, before I headed back to Ray's apartment to have ramen with him, and repeating my search for the next day.

One day when I got back to his apartment, Ray pulled out two tickets of some sort, and announced excitedly.

"What do you say that we go to Atlantic City this weekend? They have Casinos!" he exclaimed.

Exhausted, and with no energy to even think how it might sound, I told Ray that I would not go anywhere until I found a place to stay. I could tell Ray was disappointed. I felt bad for responding to his warm invitation so bluntly, especially since I knew he was just trying to cheer me up. Though Ray didn't say anything. He just quietly put the tickets away.

For the next couple of days, when he had time, Ray went on these home-hunting trips with me and provided his helpful assessments as well. It was really nice to have his company. His comments and observations often confirmed my gut feelings about those unsuitable options. When he first came along, Ray convinced me to have some reasonable lunch. Though I was not sure how he felt watching me throw up each time afterwards. So he had to give it up and just let me eat the slices of bread that I brought with me. At least the bread gave my always-over-stressed stomach an easier task to handle.

One day toward the end of August, Ray and I went to see this townhouse in a different area in Brooklyn. It was a bit far from the closest subway station. But the neighborhood was surprisingly quiet and clean. It was not like Chinatown or most other places that I had visited so far at all.

People were well dressed, professional-looking, and courteous. Birds were chirping on shadowy trees that decorated this nicely landscaped neighborhood. Houses looked nice and clean. Yards were freshly mowed with colorful flowers planted along the walkways. Everything simply felt pleasant and refreshing.

The Chinese lady who answered the door on the second floor of that townhouse told me to call her "June." She looked to be in her early 30's. She was very friendly, and spoke standard Mandarin. Her seven-year-old son was practicing music, playing a sweet and simple melody on an upright piano. The living room was spacious and was brightly lit with natural light. An elderly couple, introduced themselves as June's parents, were cooking some delicious-smelling Chinese food in the kitchen. Everyone greeted us with warm and genuine smiles on their faces.

The room for rent was cozy but not too small. It was clean and filled with sunshine that poured in through a large window at the far end of the room. I could smell the flowers' fragrance carried in by a fresh breeze from the outside. There was a regular twin-sized bed with a wrought-iron bedframe and a clean mattress, not just some dirty mattresses on the floor like in many other places. The bed lined one sidewall in the room. A small nightstand was tucked in front of the window, beside the head of the bed. And a student desk-and-chair set was set up at the foot of the bed. The room even had a closet next to the door. And it was deep enough that both my suitcases could fit inside. There was a simple telephone set on the desk.

"It is connected and ready for use." June informed me. "Of course you will have to pay for your own calls, and half of the utility costs." she further explained.

"Okay." I nodded. By now I understood that it was part of the standard package for these room rentals.

And the best part? The rent was very reasonable at only three hundred dollars a month. I was ready to take the offer on the spot. But Ray stepped in. He skillfully negotiated the rent down by another twenty dollars. As he pointed out that the location was a long 30-minute walk from the nearest subway station.

Eager to make this place mine, I took out my wallet, and handed two hundred dollars to June to hold the place. We agreed on a move-in date of September 1, which was only two days' away. After checking the room one more time in detail, I reluctantly left the apartment with Ray. I was already falling in love with this place and started to dream about my new life in that room – my room, and my new home!

Back on the street, I felt the kind of relief and joy that I had not felt since I left Beijing. It was hard to believe that was not even two weeks ago.

"Let's celebrate it!" Ray suggested cheerfully. He was probably just as relieved that my home-hunting phase was finally over.

"Yes! Let's do it." I was overjoyed and couldn't stop smiling. "No Chinese food though!" I declared. Somehow, those days that I spent in Chinatown had left a bad taste in my mouth for the food that they'd offered.

So we went to eat at a McDonald's instead.

Just two more days and I could finally settle down in New York City. I was so immersed in the joy for finding such a wonderful place. And I really wanted to relish this victory even more.

"Do you still want to go to Atlantic City?" I remembered those tickets that Ray had got, and asked him.

"Yes. Do you want to go tomorrow?" Ray was affected by how happy I was and suggested eagerly.

"Sure. Let's do it!" Nobody could be happier than I was.

That night, Ray found those tickets. And we made a day trip to Atlantic City the very next day. I even tried my hands on gambling for the first time in my life and won a couple of dollars.

"Please let me thank you with a good lunch." I announced.

Though the "good lunch" ended up being some simple and pretty cheap sandwiches from a cart right on the beach. However, it tasted like the most delicious food in the world to me.

All day long I felt lighthearted and invigorated. The ocean water was nice and warm. Though without our swimsuits, we just walked on the beach, sat on the sand, and enjoyed the sun. In a way, it almost felt like I was as carefree as I used to be when I was back home in China, way before this trip, when I had no worries in the entire world.

We took some pictures, and got them developed quickly. Later that evening after getting back to Columbia University, I put a couple of the new pictures in a letter home. I told my family the great news that I had found a wonderful new home now. I wrote down my new address and June's phone number. And I asked them to write me there soon.

September 1, my big move-in day finally came.

I dragged Ray to go with me one more time. We went to John's place first, got my two large suitcases. Then I practiced a new skill to flag down a yellow cab for the first time in my life. We put the suitcases into the cab's trunk, which filled up the entire trunk space. I realized then just how much I had missed my luggage for the last several days, and was so delighted to be reunited with them again.

We then headed over to Shirley's dorm to pick up my small suitcase.

It felt tremendous to be rejoined with all my worldly possessions. I sat in the back seat of the yellow cab, held my small suitcase and my red bag on my lap. Hugging them tight for the rest of the trip to my new home, I finally felt at peace and complete.

At last, I moved into my own place in New York.

My homeless days were officially over and behind me. Life became wonderful again!

NEW YORK CITY

*The question isn't who is going to let me;
it's who is going to stop me.*

~ Ayn Rand

CHAPTER TEN

September 1, 1990

EVEN THOUGH RAY VOLUNTEERED TO STAY AND HELP ME UNPACK, I insisted that he go back to Manhattan with the taxi. I wanted to savor the feeling of finally being in my own place with all my belongings.

At long last, I was alone, in my own room. I closed the door, looked around the room, and everything in it, cherishing the moment. The last two weeks of having no place to call home and being unable to feel completely at ease took an enormous toll on me. The pain and shock could be best described as 刻骨铭心 (felt like carved in the bones and etched in the heart). Even though I was so grateful that I didn't have to live on the street (or any other public places) because of the help from John, Martin, Shirley, and Ray.

Two weeks wasn't a very long time in most circumstances. But to me, those two weeks felt like an eternity. So many important pieces of myself, including some core foundation blocks of my being, got broken down and stripped away. I had lost so much: my confidence, my dignity, my self-image, my sense of security and belonging, not to mention my family, my home, and my friends. Like my suitcases, those essential parts of me were forgotten in so many ways, left littered around, unattended. I wandered aimlessly in this city, focused only on one mission in order to survive - finding a place to live, and finding my new home here in NYC and in the

USA. There were days that I did not even think about anything else but that mission, forgetting about my suitcases and everything in them. Until this moment, when I could finally breathe.

And now, with all my property here with me, though laying around the room haphazardly, I felt as if I had also picked up some of those lost pieces of myself, and gathered them around me again.

But I wondered how I could stitch my life back together. Even though I had my things back, *I* had changed. I was no longer the same ignorant and naive girl in so many ways. These pieces of me could never fit back the way they did. And I could never go back to the way I was. So, what would this new put-back-together me look like? Who would this new *me* be? Now that I was finally settled in New York City, in the USA, and ready to start my new life here. What would this life be like?

I sat down on the carpeted floor, opened my suitcases, and started to take the items out. Everything reminded me of the time as it was packed in, when I was back home in Beijing. Except back then I was with my family. And now I was in New York City, half a world away, all by myself.

I held out the pillowcases that Mom picked out for me, grabbed the blanket with the tiger print that Dad put inside the suitcase, and buried my face in them. Sucked in their scent deeply, I could smell whiffs of the familiar odor of the mothball from the wooden storage case, scent of home, of Mom, Dad, and *Gege*.

Eyes closed, I imagined that I was still home with them. While the dumplings were cooking in our tiny kitchen, and the TV was playing in my parents' bedroom. I almost felt like I could smell the cooking and wished that I could eat more of those delicious dumplings again. After a long while, I put the blanket and one of the pillowcases down on my new bed reluctantly, and continued unpacking.

I took out the pots, the chopping knife, the chopsticks, other cooking and dining ware, and put them into the kitchen drawer that June emptied out for me to use. I carefully hung my clothes in the closet, appreciated the hangers that June had thoughtfully left in there for me. I marveled at the reasons why we didn't have closets in China, and at the luxury that I had one now, all to myself.

Pretty soon I got to the bottom of the last suitcase. The two dictionaries were the last items in there – leaning against each other, spine to spine. Daddy's face seemed to be right in front of my eyes, smiling and telling me, "See, no damage to the pages." I took them out. They weighed heavy in my hands, just as how my heart felt at that moment.

Every item reminded me of my family, of my friends, of home. How I wished that I was there with them still. As I was putting the dictionaries onto my new desk, a black and white picture fell out. It was a portrait of Mom, taken when she was young. Looking at Mom's beautiful face, my tears finally rolled down my cheeks. And it was like a broken dam, once started, it would not stop.

In my tears, I continued to set up my new room, my new home. I left my red diary notebook on the desk. "I will write down some of the memorable events soon." I reminded myself.

When it was all done, I put the now almost-empty suitcases inside the closet. Then I stood in front of the opened closet door, relishing the moment. On that eye-level long rod, hung my long heavy coat, my pink sweater, my shirts, jeans, skirts, pants, jackets, and more sweaters.

Without thinking, I opened my arms wide, gathered all of the clothes into a bundle, I hugged them tight. I wished that they were Mom, Dad, and *Gege*. I wished that I had hugged my family before I left home, and that I could have taken their warmth and scents with me.

But hugging was just not part of our custom, not even within the family.

Though now in my own room with my door closed, I could hug these belongings that I had brought from home with me, and pretend that they were my family.

Each of these items was picked, packed, and touched by Mom, Dad, and *Gege*, with love. They were all that I had now, all that I had in this world. And suddenly, I realized just how deeply I missed these items in the past two weeks, and how deeply I missed my family at this moment.

These material possessions of mine, and only these things, were my family and my companion now.

When my tears finally ran dry, I went to the bathroom to wash my face. My reflection in the mirror looked familiar, yet different somehow. I used to be so carefree and so untroubled. The *me* in the mirror now seemed to have more on her mind, and more mature-looking. I couldn't pinpoint the change. But I wondered just how much more I would continue to adjust, grow, and reinvent myself in this new world. And would that ever stop?

Though more practical thoughts grabbed my attention pretty soon. I needed to think about what to do next. The sun was already halfway down to the horizon. I took out my wallet and counted all the money I had left in there. It was just under sixty dollars. Along with that one-thousand-dollar check from Wendy that I had no idea on how to use.

But as I looked around again of my room, joy and pride filled my heart. I had found my own place, and I had finally moved in.

"I have a home now, in America! Mom and Dad will be delighted!"

I propped Mom's picture against the wall on the desk, so she could see the entire room. She would be so proud of me. They would all be.

After the past two weeks of being homeless, this new home of mine felt like heaven on earth. I had to share this terrific news with my family.

I sat down at my new desk, picked up the handset of my new phone, and made my very first call from my new home to my old home. Mom picked up the phone right away. She was so glad and relieved that I finally called again. She had not yet received my letter, and had been worried sick about me. I told her that I was doing great, and had just moved into my own place now. I gave her the address and June's telephone number. I told her that my letter was on its way and that I hoped to see their letters soon and often. I quickly added that everything was marvelous and that I would write more detailed letters soon. I hung up the phone just before we hit the 3-minute mark.

Then I made a second call to Connor in California. So I could give him the same updates and to check in and see how he was doing. It was nice that I didn't have to be as rushed with this call. I learned that he was doing really well. Before we hang up, we set the date when he would call me back, in a few days' time.

It felt wonderful to hear their voices, and it made my heart swell with happiness. I held back my tears, simply enjoyed our brief moments on the phone together, and reveled in every second of them.

Now that I felt so much better emotionally after those two quick calls, I needed to think about refueling my body with dinner. And I also need to get a pillow to sleep on. So I asked June for the closest store to get these items. She told me about a small mom-and-pop grocery shop nearby where I could get all that I needed. She also informed me that this was an Italian neighborhood. So the store had a lot of Italian food, some even similar to our Chinese food.

A few minutes later, for the first time in the USA, I left my new home and walked outside with just my wallet. I could never get tired of looking at the beautiful streets of my new quiet neighborhood. I felt so blessed and lighthearted. And I realized that this was my first trip-out since leaving China that I did not have my big red canvas bag on me.

The air outside was jovial. The neighborhood was infused by fragrance from flowers. The sidewalk was shaded by mature trees besides the road, with birds singing and butterflies dancing in the air. Three-story townhomes, like the one I now lived in, were built with red bricks. Their yards encircled by white picket fences and green lawns. It looked pristine with brightly colored flowers decorated the sides of the walkways. It felt like I was in a movie. How lucky was I to find such a perfect place like this and to make it my own new home.

The grocery store was not far. And it was easy to find. Though how it worked was a new concept to me. Things were just laid out on these shelves and even cold open cabinets. Anyone could simply walk up and pick whatever they wanted, and put back anything they didn't like. That was completely different from the stores in China, where all merchandise was behind the counter, and we had to ask the clerk for anything that we were interested in taking a look at or purchase.

"Hmmm, I guess people here are much more honest and trust-worthy. And the stores don't need to worry about things getting stolen as much." I thought.

The owner of the shop was an elderly gentleman with grey hair and kind eyes. He greeted me cordially with curiosity.

"He must know all the regular shoppers and probably wonders where I'd come from." I thought with a little silent chuckle to myself, "Well, he will be seeing me regularly from now on."

I took my time to browse, read the labels and checked the prices. Many items had unfamiliar packaging and it was hard for me to guess what they actually were. There were even some canned food that had cat or dog pictures on them.

"Do they eat cat and dog meat?" I was really confused. It took me a while before I realized that the shelf had a whole bunch of food and toys *for* cats and dogs. "Wow!" I thought, "We have nothing like this in China." I made a mental note to myself to tell my family about this. Back then, few people had pets in China. And if they did, they fed them leftovers from the kitchen table. At this moment in that store, I was just glad that I didn't mistake those cans for people food, and put any into my basket.

At the end, I found the most essential things for what I needed, and followed the short line to pay for my purchase. The stash of assorted items cost me over twenty dollars. I walked away with both of my hands full. I got myself a new pillow (It was so light and spongy!), some ramen noodles, a small pack of rice, some vegetables, meat, fruits, salt, oil, and a few other items.

As I was leaving the store, I saw a black stretch limousine parked on the street not far away. Wow. I had never seen a long car like that except in the movies. I was even more impressed by this neighborhood and glad that this was my new home.

"Is this even for real?" I pinched myself to make sure that it was not just a dream.

About a block away from home, on the sidewalk in front of me, three teenage boys were throwing a football with each other. This was a sport that I had never seen before. They stopped playing politely when I got close and waited for me to pass. As I walked by, one of them said, "Pretty. I like pretty Chinese girls."

My heart skipped a beat. Although I didn't stop or change my pace. I was surprised that I actually understood him, and that he thought I was pretty.

THAT NIGHT AND the next day, I sat at my new desk for hours at a time and kept on writing. I wrote a whole bunch of letters: to Connor, Faye, Chengyun, my cousins, my teachers, Connor's parents, several other friends, and another letter home.

I told everyone that I had arrived in New York City. That I had visited Chinatown and taken the New York City subway, and that they were not as scary as I thought. I shared that NYU was beautiful with its large buildings, the appealing Washington Square Park, and its great stone arch. I wrote that the buildings in Manhattan were majestic, tall, with beautiful designs, fancy elevators, and clean and shiny floors. I mentioned that the school was right next to the famous Broadway Street. I reported that I had found a great place to live, had my own room, with my own closet and telephone. And I announced that my new neighborhood was super nice, quiet, fragrant and charming just like in the movies.

I shared all the great news and none of the bad. Except in the ones to Connor and Faye. I told the two of them about some of the challenges I had faced, in light strokes. And that now I was in a perfect place and quite content with the situation.

I told everyone my new address and June's telephone number. I told them that I would write more soon again. And "Please," I requested, "please write back to me." as I missed them so dearly.

As I wrote, I remembered the good old times I spent with them, and my tears would start flowing again. Then I switched to write in my journal instead. All the hardship, my homeless days, the loneliness, the sad dreams, and the tears. I wrote in my journal until I stopped crying. Then I would wash my face, take a breather. Before I sat back down again, and continue with the next chirpy letter.

Monday was the "Labor Day" holiday in the US, so I enjoyed my new home for another free day. As I wrote more in my journal, I realized that ever since I moved into my new home, that back-at-Beijing-home sad dream had stopped its nightly visit. And that I no longer woke myself up in tears every morning.

INSIDE THE FRONT cover of my journal, I decided to write down a few words to remind myself to be strong, and self-reliant as Mom always taught me to be. Now that I was no longer a spoiled baby at home or a sheltered college student. I needed to show myself, and the world, what I was made of. And what I could accomplish in this new world of NYU and the USA.

There, I wrote in Chinese –

忍耐与坚强　　(Resilience and fortitude)
在最难的时候　(At the toughest times)
能始终不移地　(The one who would faithfully)
支持你的：　　(Support you and stand by you:)
只有你　　　　(Is only you)
自己！　　　　(Yourself!)

The next morning, I decided that I would try to see if I could cash the check from Wendy. As it really bugged me that I still owe June part of the rent. I went to the neighborhood bank as June suggested. But I was told that I would need a second "ID card", besides my passport, in order for me to open a bank account there. Only after I opened such an account, they said, could I deposit that check into it, before I could take that money out to use.

"What is an ID?" I asked. Not certain if we had anything equivalent in China. Since I was going to be a student at NYU, they said that I should be getting a Student ID from the school. And I could use that to open a bank account. So I needed to go and ask NYU about how to get this Student ID card.

As I turned to leave the bank, I saw an Asian girl standing at the door, staring at me.

"Are you Chinese?" I was hopeful and asked her.

She nodded eagerly with a happy smile. We started talking and I was ecstatic that I had found someone like myself.

Her name was Cindy. She arrived in New York from a southern Chinese province just three days ago. She was staying with her uncle, who told her to come to the bank and open an account, and to go get her Social Security card, all by herself.

Cindy was terrified about the idea to do any of these things on her own. But she did not know what else she could do, as her uncle was busy at his job and didn't have time to help her with these things. I remembered how I felt when I was on the streets here for the first time by myself. So I told her that I was happy to help her if she'd like. I could tell that my offer took a huge load off her mind, as her smile grew even wider. She nodded her head quickly. Since Martin had also told me that I would need to get a Social Security card, I figured we could go together to get that done.

I helped Cindy to check with the bank first. And got the same answer as they gave me earlier, that she also needed another ID. So she would have to wait as well. We then left the bank together for our next stop – to apply for our Social Security cards.

"I heard it is in midtown Manhattan." I told her about this government office where we needed to go visit next, as I led her toward the subway station. "We will take the subway to get there." I informed her.

She suddenly stopped dead in her tracks. I was surprised when I realized that she had fallen behind, and looked back to find her.

"Something wrong?" I asked.

"Subway? The New York City subway?" She looked terrified.

I couldn't help but smile. Remembering my own reaction upon hearing about taking the subway for the very first time, and how scared I was back then.

"Yes. It's okay. Trust me!"

All day long, Cindy stuck by my side, like a little sister. Although I learned that we were about the same age as we shared more information about ourselves with each other. After applying for the Social Security cards, we tried to apply for work permits as well but got rejected. Since we came to the US for education, we did not qualify to work outside of the schools during the school year.

Cindy looked at me as if I were her savior and hero. She listened to my broken English with so much envy and wonderment on her face. Spending time with her reminded me so much of how I was myself, just merely two weeks ago, when I first arrived at this city. It was amazing to realize how far I had come since then. I told Cindy that I was in her exact spot just a few days prior and that she would be fine too, very soon.

O UR ENGLISH AS a Second Language (ESL) class for the new Teaching Assistants (TAs) also started. Though it was only for a couple of hours each day. I was glad to have a regular schedule and a purpose to my day. I was even more thrilled to meet a few other new students from China there. One of them was Quinn. Quinn was a bubbly and friendly lady, who also came from Beijing. We became instant friends. And I was glad to learn that we were both attending the Biology Department as well.

Each day, when the ESL class was over, we would say goodbye to each other and take our separate trains to go home. I was pleased to attend the ESL classes, grateful for meeting these new friends, and having a safe place to practice my English. Even though I felt quite embarrassed and inadequate most of the time in those classes. My hour-long commute was also becoming a comfortable routine, even if I was always on those trains by myself.

Soon, our school was finally about to start too.

By this time, I was counting my pennies and had borrowed $20 from my new friend Quinn already. I promised June that I would pay her all the rest of the deposit and my rent as soon as I had cash. I had showed her my scholarship offering letter and that thousand-dollar check from Wendy to prove that I could afford to live there. I had also tried to go to a couple of other banks, both near home and around the school. But I was always told the same thing – that I needed a Student ID to open a bank account. I had asked NYU about this ID card and learned that I had to wait for school registration to get it.

The registration day couldn't have come soon enough.

That morning, I arrived at school early, and stood eagerly in the long line of waiting students. I was fascinated by how orderly and patiently these students waited in line. And I was amazed by how startlingly beautiful looking many of the students were. It made me even more self-conscious about how different I looked, and how awkward and out of place I felt.

I was also stunned to see some students would sit on the floor in the hallways. That was another sight that I had never seen in China. I guessed that it made sense since the floor here looked spotless and smooth. And most people washed their clothes in washing machines instead of hand-washing them. So it was not as big of a chore if their clothes got dirty quickly. I was so affected by such observations that I wrote in my letters home extensively. "The floors are made of shiny marbles or covered by carpets, so nice and clean. Not at all like the grey dull concrete floors which was ubiquitous in our buildings and homes." I exclaimed.

I was also surprised by how the streets of NYC and the buildings around NYU were suddenly filled with so many people, students and teachers alike. It was such a stark contrast compared to the previous few weeks, when it was so quiet in those buildings as if they were ghost towns. And it was refreshing to see how brightly and colorfully people were dressed, unlike the greyish clothes that was everywhere in China.

When I got to the front of the registration line, I was given a list of things that I needed to provide for my registration. Besides all the documents, official letters, and my passport that I had piled onto their desk, I was also asked to pay a registration fee of $462.

"Wait, what?"

Nowhere had any of the letters from NYU ever mentioned that I had to pay for school. I thought my scholarship would cover all the costs. I pointed out that big oversight from the school. But apparently it was non-negotiable.

"No money, no registration." they told me.

I pulled out the thousand-dollar check from Wendy. It had become my last resource for everything that I had yet to pay. But they wouldn't take that either. Because it was not for the right amount, and it was not addressed to the school.

What was I going to do?

The girl behind the desk suggested sympathetically, "Can you ask your parents for the money?"

"My *parents*?!"

The parents who had already given me absolutely everything they had and more? My incredulous expression probably alarmed or even amused her, and she added quickly,

"Maybe ask a friend then?"

But what friend? I reluctantly left the registration office and figured that I'd go and ask Martin.

Martin listened to my new dilemma. Without hesitation, he pulled out his checkbook and wrote a check to the school to cover that $462 for me.

No time to worry about yet another debt that I had to repay soon. I thanked him and rushed back to the registration office again. Another hour later, I was at the front of the line for the second time. They accepted Martin's check without any question and directed me to a photo booth. Few minutes later, I was handed my very first Student ID in the USA. All shiny and new, with me wearing that same pink sweater that I wore to the US embassy just over a month ago, with an almost grimacing expression on my face this time.

With my new Student ID card on hand, I rushed over to the closest bank near school. I showed them my new card and my passport and handed them the thousand-dollar check, which by now looked quite sad and worn on the edges. Without any more issues, my first bank account was opened. Wendy's check was finally deposited.

Two days later I went back to the same bank and took out $500 in cash, and left the other half on the checking account. I found Martin and wrote him the first check that I had ever written for $480, to pay him back for that registration fee and thank him for everything he had done for me.

"Great! Now I have just $20 on my account left." I thought.

But I felt relieved that I cleared that debt first, and found a small way to show Martin my appreciation for his help. Then I found Quinn, and gave her back the $20 cash that I borrowed from her. Once I got home that night, I handed June over $400 from the rest of the cash to cover what I owed her.

It felt tremendous to have all these new debts settled. And I decided to go to McDonald's to celebrate it, by buying two Big Mac's with their special Two-for-Two deal. Anything more would have been too luxurious to contemplate. Since I was now back down to just about $60 left, and it needed to last me until my first paycheck.

But it felt great that I had officially become a student in the USA, with a shiny new Student ID card to prove it.

I smiled to myself as I sank my teeth into that juicy burger.

Chapter Eleven

School finally started. So did our classes.

We had our first official meeting with all the Teaching Assistants (TAs) in our department. Newbies like myself, together with senior graduate students who had been there for a year or longer. I finally got to meet some other Chinese students in our department as well.

All the new TAs including those whom I had met at the ESL class got assignments to teach freshman classes. But somehow I got selected to teach the genetics discussion class for junior undergraduate students, working together with three senior TAs in our Ph.D. program. The assignment made me a little nervous.

Steve, the coordinator of our TA group for the genetics class, was a nice American guy. Francesco was a friendly and humorous guy from Italy. Not much older than myself, both of them were third-year Ph.D. students in our department. And lastly, Kim, a student from Korea who seemed to be always somewhere else instead of at our meetings. Steve paired me up with Francesco, and left himself with the tough task of tracking down the elusive Kim.

Francesco had a round face, kind eyes, and very curly hair. He noticed right away that my English was very limited and that I didn't talk much. So he volunteered to do all the talking and teaching in our class. He suggested that I took charge of the homework and tests. So my job was to prepare them and grade them. He had been teaching this class for a couple of years now, he explained, and that it would be easy for him to teach if that was okay with me.

Okay with me? That was better than anything I could think of. I was ecstatic. Such tasks were a lot less stressful for me, compared to talking to people. We learned to read and write English for many years in China but didn't have as much opportunity to converse with it. Francesco's suggestion brought me a huge relief. I nodded quickly and gave him a heartfelt smile as my form of a "Thank You."

That afternoon I went to the first genetics lecture. I was awed by the large size of the theater-style lecture hall. It was packed with over a hundred and twenty students. Some couldn't even find a seat and had to stand along the wall. I guessed that NYU must be a much bigger school than USTC.

When I entered USTC, we had 777 undergraduate students in all the 13 departments across the University, with 111 girls and 666 boys. A fact that was shared with us at the welcoming ceremony on the first night of school. There were about 50 students in our Biology Department that year, including Faye, Ray, Stacy, Jonathan and Shirley. And it was really nice that the fifty of us got to know each other pretty well, as we took most of our classes together, for at least four out of those five years.

Looking around that room at the NYU genetics class, and all the eager students in it, I was a bit overwhelmed. There were so many students there, and half of them would be *my* students. They all looked so lovely and hungry to learn. Many of them looked older than myself. Although somehow in my head, I called them collectively "these kids."

Would I be able to teach them? Would I be able to help them with this class? To add value to them? And not to be a burden to Francesco and Steve? Would they laugh at me? At my broken English? At how different and out of place I looked? I had a lot of questions and was quite nervous about this assignment.

When the class was over, I went to the front of the classroom and introduced myself to the professor.

Professor Murphy was very nice. She was happy to meet me and to learn that I had just attended her class. She asked me a few basic questions and was pleased with my answers. She handed me a thick and heavy textbook for the class. "A gift to you." she announced. And she dismissed my concern about my limited English skills,

"I am glad to have you here. Don't worry, you will be just fine." She said kindly.

What a nice professor! I walked away delighted. Holding that new heavy textbook tight to my chest, I felt relieved and grateful for my job as a TA in her class.

WHEN MY OWN classes started, however, I realized that school was not just a cheerful place. There were a lot of hard work ahead. We had a heavy load of classes. Though biochemistry was the worst. And for some reason, I was the only Chinese student who elected the microbiology class, which was very demanding as well, with its complicated Latin vocabulary for those micro-organisms.

For most lectures of these two classes, I had a really hard time understanding the professors and the lectures. The classrooms for our classes were huge. And no matter where I sat, I could hardly see anything that was written on the board. I tried to take notes. But most of the time, I just stared at the professor the entire class. Trying as hard as I did, I still could not understand much, let alone write anything down for notes. The books were over $100 apiece. There was no way that I could afford to purchase even a single copy of them.

How would this work? I was at a loss.

And I was not alone.

There were five new Chinese graduate students in our department this year, even though ten were admitted. I guessed that the other five couldn't make it somehow, even with full-scholarships. That was not too surprising, given how hard it was to come to the USA for all of us. In fact, someone said that the school was glad that only half of us made it. As there were concerns that maybe too many students from China would be risky in a way. That it might cause some kind of imbalance in the graduate program. And that it had not been proven that Chinese students could adapt well in an American university like NYU yet.

Regardless, the five of us lucky ones bonded well. We were happy that the school had accepted all of us. We found a couple of other Chinese students in our department who came in the years ahead of us. One of them was also from USTC, who had graciously offered to lend me his used textbook from the previous year. We soaked up every bit of knowledge and experience they shared with us.

"Go to the library to read the textbooks. They won't let you check them out, but you can read them there. The basement of the library has individual cubicles that are quiet and great for studying."

I followed their advice closely, started to study with an intensity that I had never had. I was eager to find a way to catch up with the teachers and the classes.

I also learned that almost all the other Chinese students lived in Queens, a different suburb of New York from Brooklyn. Some senior students who valued convenience and time more, and didn't mind to pay higher rent for smaller places, lived right there in Manhattan. Basically, I was pretty much on my own in Brooklyn.

The benefit of solitary living was the greater control I had with my schedule. Most mornings, I would walk thirty minutes from my home to the subway station and take the train to school as early as possible. If I didn't have classes in the morning, I would head over to the library directly. I would find a textbook for one of my classes, and carry it down to the basement to study. I would get myself a desk, lay down the textbooks, my dictionaries, my notebook, and try to read.

It felt like I didn't know at least half of the words in those textbooks, such as all those amino acids, the amines, the ethers, the ketones, the enzymes, bacteria and viruses, etc. So I wrote those new words down in my notebook, and found their translations in the dictionaries. I then wrote the Chinese names next to the English ones, before I try again to read the sentences and paragraphs to see if I could understand them better.

I aimed to go over each chapter at least three times. First, just to write down the new words so I could translate them. Then I replaced the English words with their translated Chinese words, and read the chapter again. And by the third time, I tried to make sense of what the book was teaching us.

I found that if I could find time to go over each chapter once or twice before class, then I might be able to catch a couple of the new words during the lectures. Though still not comprehending much of concepts that the professors were trying to teach us, I was at least making some progress instead of staying completely lost.

Most of the days I spent the bulk of my time in the lecture halls. Whether it was attending my own classes, or "teaching" the genetics classes. At those genetics classes I just observed and learned from the way how Francesco taught them. And I left each class with big stacks of paper to grade. Slowly, Francesco started to ask me to participate more in the classroom dialog and challenged me to interact more with the students as well.

Francesco was very funny, super smart, and the students just loved him. He also invited me to use the laboratory where he was doing his research, to grade homework and tests there. This way he could help if I needed it. And I wouldn't have to always take thick stacks of paper home each night. So, my days went by fairly quickly as I rushed around from the classrooms, to Francesco's lab, and the library.

WHEN WE FINALLY got our first paychecks, I was thrilled. I tore open the envelope anxiously and took out the folded paper inside. This was the first time in my life that I got a paycheck. I scanned the page quickly - there - at the bottom of the page, was a printed check. And my name was on it.

And the dollar amount printed there was almost $1,400! Wow! My heart leaped with joy. That was a lot more money than I expected. I was elated.

The original offering letter from NYU said that we would get $8,800 a year stipend in exchange for the TA work. So in my mind, each month I could expect a check for about $733. But this check was almost twice as much.

The senior students explained that the stipend was adjusted for inflation, and our new department chairman gave us all a nice rise on top of that. In addition, because the school year was less than nine months long, that was why we got paid more each month during that time.

Okay, so we wouldn't get paid over the breaks. And that was something to be planned for later. I made a mental note to myself.

"Also, as international students, we don't need to pay taxes." the senior students further explained. Though I really didn't care what the reasons were, I was just overjoyed for the extra "bonus" money that we got now.

And I needed to save everything possible, so I could pay back the rest of the borrowed money soon. I figured that with this income, I should be able to save nearly $1,000 each month. Then I could be debt-free in a couple of months, and send some money home when I saved more.

I kept that in mind when I went shopping again at my neighborhood grocery store. It was pretty much the only place that I spent any money, except for the subway fare and my rent. Carefully screening all the price tags, I found the cheapest food there.

There was some cheap lunch meat. "It is still meat, for human to eat, right?" I reasoned as I put a thick package of sliced bologna into my basket. Wow, the bread was already sliced. How convenient. I took one of the cheapest packs of sliced bread that was on sale. I picked up a couple of tomatoes for vegetables, and got a bottle of tomato sauce called ketchup, which looked like what I saw in those sandwiches that some American students ate. I got eggs for more protein, and of course, at a few cents a pack, I added a bunch of ramen noodle packets in my basket.

I calculated it – with these essential items, and maybe a special treat once or twice a month – I could have a fairly balanced diet for under $50 a month. The subway tokens cost me just as much to go to school each day. And my half of the utility bill was close to that amount as well.

So, even though I had a phone in my own room, I couldn't afford to use it too much. Calls to Beijing were rare, at over three dollars a minute, I would have to cut off at around 55-second mark. or 1:55, if somehow the first minute slipped by before I could wrap it up.

But I needed to call California even if it cost me. I wanted to talk to Connor each week. There were other friends who were scattered around in the US and Canada with whom I wanted to stay in touch as well.

All the long-distance calls were expensive. And the three-hour delay for California meant that I had to wait until late at night or the weekend to make those calls to talk to Connor, and occasionally, to Faye as well. But I still looked forward to each call with them, and never wanted to cut them short.

And I wrote letters, a lot of letters. At least the stamps were not very expensive. In my letters home or to my elders, I would still only tell them the good news so they wouldn't have to worry about me. But to my friends, especially to those who wanted to come to the USA to study as well, I started to tell them more about the difficult truth. That life here could be quite lonely. It could be hard. The culture shock was real. And schools and classes could be very difficult.

I didn't know if that made any difference for them. And I didn't know whether it would have helped me if someone had told me such truth before I left China. But I hoped that whatever I shared could help others to be better prepared than I was.

"At least," I told those who were ready to go apply for their visas, "make sure you ask your school to help you arrange a place to stay, *before* you get on the plane to come here."

I N MOST EVENINGS after my classes, I would go down to the basement of the library to study, and to avoid the rush-hour train ride home.

One such night, I took a break and went to the bathroom to freshen up. As I was heading back to my desk in rushed and determined steps, while still thinking about the chapter that I was studying, when "*Bam!*" I walked fast and hard, right into a super clean, unmarked, and heavy glass wall.

The collision between my forehead and the glass was so severe that the thick glass vibrated, and my forehead hurt like hell. (So bad, in fact, that about a decade later, it showed up on an x-ray film of my neck. My very experienced chiropractic doctor declared that he could tell that I had a severe car accident over 10 years ago that I didn't know about.)

At the time of the incident though, all I knew was that there was a loud thump from the impact. So loud that I instinctively looked around quickly, to make sure that the noise didn't startle many others in the quiet library. I was relieved that the glass was heavy and solid, and my forehead did not break it. But my head was clobbered. To the point that even though I went back to my carrel desk, I did not sit down for long. I got back up again after just a couple of seconds and went back to the bathroom.

Remembering a tip on treating burn accidents with cold water, I turned on the faucet and splashed cold water onto my forehead. Even though the accident was not a burn, I hoped that it would cool down the area, and somehow control the extent of the bleeding under the skin.

Still, as I looked into the mirror over the sink, I saw a spreading redness right in the dead center of my forehead. It continued to grow in size and brighten in color. And it was not just a discoloration. A lump formed quickly and continued to swell, despite the cold water that I kept on splashing over the heated skin. The swelling started to protrude from my forehead like a red tennis ball, forming and growing, as I watched my reflection in the mirror, horrified.

A student came out of a bathroom stall. She looked at me and noticed the swelling lump that was now covering almost a third of my big forehead immediately. She got concerned and asked if I was okay.

I mumbled "Yeah, I am fine." back to her, while continued the cold water treatment on my injury. Eventually, I realized that I had to leave the bathroom at some point. So I grabbed a piece of paper towel, folded it up, wet it with cold water, and plastered it over the affected area above my eyes.

When I felt that I had done everything I could, I headed back to my seat. With that wet paper towel held over the lump with one hand, I stuck out the other arm in front of myself like a blind person. I walked at a much slower pace, to make sure that I wouldn't walk into another invisible wall again.

Realizing that no more study was possible that night, I gathered my books and headed home early. There were a lot more people at this hour of the evening everywhere: on the street, waiting on the subway platform, and inside the subway itself. For the entire trip home, I held that paper towel over the lump with one hand, and kept myself steady and my bag safe with the other.

And how I wished for some special power of invisibility, while trying to ignore the throbbing pain radiating from the center of my head. I averted the curious looks from other travelers. I made it home eventually and then spent considerably more time in the bathroom to inspect the degree of the damage.

At least the lump had finally stopped growing. Now a very angry, red-colored, half-moon-shaped bulge stood prominently on the center of my forehead, with a tight patch of warm skin stretched over it. It seemed to be mocking me and challenging me on what I could do about it. I sighed. Staring at it in the mirror certainly was not going to cure it or make it disappear. I guessed that I had no choice but to accept "It is what it is." and move on to do whatever I had to do.

The next morning, I found that Cadillac baseball cap that Dad had gifted me before I left home. Carefully lifted the band over the giant lump, I put the cap on until it covered the entire lump, sitting low over my eyes. I checked myself in the bathroom mirror one more time, and let out a deep breath. It was the best I could do to conceal my foolish accident.

I felt weird the entire way to school, partially from the discomfort of the cap pressing down on the lump and hurting it, and partially from feeling very self-conscious about wearing that cap at all.

At our morning genetics class, Francesco got curious about the reason that I suddenly decided to wear a baseball cap, and a Cadillac cap at that. So he asked me about it. My face turned red. I tried not to share the embarrassing story, which made he even more perplexed. Eventually I gave up and reluctantly told him about the incident from the night before. He started to chuckle and made me take off the cap so he could see the lump. When I showed him, he laughed so hard that I started laughing as well. Eventually I had to show all the students in that class the big badge of honor on my forehead.

The good news was that by this point, I had already become very comfortable with our students, and I had embarrassed myself enough times by making all kinds of mistakes in class that I didn't have to feel too ashamed for this anymore.

Over the next couple of weeks, as my injury slowly healed, the skin on my forehead went through the spectrum of the rainbow colors. And the lump slowly retracted back to the flattened plain of my forehead. A nice American student in my class suggested that I could use some makeup to cover the bruise. But wearing makeup was also foreign to me. And I was not ready to waste money on something that my cap could cover without any additional cost.

So, that Cadillac cap had become a constant part of my wardrobe for those weeks. With the exceptions when I was in our genetics classes or in Francesco's lab. There, I could take off the cap and let the lump air out, without worrying about the constant stares and questions. Since Francesco had already made sure that not only our students, but also everyone in his lab, learned about my big secret as well.

Chapter Twelve

With all the mistakes, and all the embarrassments, there was a lot of progress too. And pretty soon, I was getting into a rhythm – a busy, stressful, yet predictable and comfortable routine.

I was still dazzled by how stunning many of the "foreigners" looked. Though I started to realize that *I* was actually the "foreigner" here, and I had my own merits as well. I loved my students and made friends with some of them. Though I felt relaxed and comfortable talking to the girls, my face always turned red when I talked to the guys in my classes.

Still, I recognized that I had a lot more in common with other TAs, especially my fellow first-year TAs from China. Even though all of them were older than myself and they were all married. They treated me like a little sister, which was quite nice and gave me a huge advantage to learn from their life experiences.

My English skill continued to improve too, however slow it seemed. I was able to take more notes during some classes now. And my students appeared to understand me much better when I tried to explain some important topics about their homework or tests. Francesco started to notice my progress and asked me to go over some common mistakes on their homework or tests during our classes. He even joked that I could start teaching those classes pretty soon myself. But I was still scared of teaching the entire class and was relieved as he continued to lead the discussions. I just kept on learning from him. My confidence in teaching started to grow and I realized that this was something that I really enjoyed doing.

Though when each school day was over, I still dreaded leaving the group, as I headed toward a different subway station all by myself. I envied the other friends who took the train together each day. Although I was still grateful for my beautiful neighborhood tremendously.

IN THE MIDST of all that, without telling my new friends, I celebrated my 23rd birthday quietly on my own on a weekend. I cooked an instant noodle dinner as Mom always prepared noodles on our birthdays to bring "good fortune and long life." I even added two poached eggs in the soup the way Mom always did.

I was glad to receive several birthday greeting cards in the mail from family and friends. And I was happily surprised to unveil my new Social Security card from an official envelope that day as well.

"Does this mean that the United States of America officially welcomes me now? And is this an official birthday present for me?" I chuckled to myself.

I wrote more in my journal that day, about what I had done and the life I had now. I wrote about the application packets that I had NYU sent out to *Gege*, my cousins and my friends. I hoped that it could help them with their pursuits to come to the US, and help me to have more friends around. I wrote about the food that I had to throw out, because I was only looking at the price tags without paying attention to their expiration dates. And I wrote about how much I missed my friends and family, and how lonely and miserable I felt by myself.

I knew I shouldn't feel that way but I was still sad to be all by myself in my room all day, while hearing the happy laughter from June's family. Connor promised that he would call. So all day long I was afraid of missing his call and stayed near the telephone the entire time. But the phone did not ring, not until close to midnight when he finally called. Just hearing his voice was enough to draw my tears out. I wished that I was not alone, that I had his company, or any company, for that special day.

So when I went back to school after that weekend, when my new best friend, Quinn, suggested that I moved closer to her, I became tempted.

Quinn was several years older than me and had been married for a few years. She had to leave her husband behind when she got the opportunity to come to NYU. She was now working on getting him a spousal visa to come and join her, but "That can take months if not years." she told me wistfully.

I also learned that Quinn had health issues when she was younger, and almost died from it. But she survived and had been well for over a decade. I admired her inner strength and her youthful spirit, ever so cheerful in our group. She was always willing to share her experience and wisdom with me, giving me a different perspective, and a lot to think about.

Though when there were just the two of us, Quinn admitted that she felt lonely often and missed her family and her husband dearly. And that she cried a lot in private, just like me. Our friendship continued to grow, and she continued to suggest that I moved closer to her. With that, my resolve about staying in my wonderful home and my lovely neighborhood started to erode.

And Quinn wasn't the only one who wanted me to be closer.

Connor and Faye also urged me to apply for a transfer to his school in LA. So "We could be together again." Connor enticed. And Faye agreed. Faye was attending a school across town from Connor's, and she liked the idea for me to move to LA too.

"We would be close enough to visit each other often." she nudged me on.

Their invitations delighted me. I started the process eagerly by getting names of a few professors at Connor's school and wrote letters to them. In those letters, I explained why I wanted to be considered for a position as a Teaching or Research Assistant in their labs. And that I would love to transfer to their graduate program very soon. I sent out those letters quickly, then I waited, and waited, for their responses.

Progress on moving closer to Quinn was a lot faster though. One day at the end of September, Quinn excitedly showed me an ad for a rental room that was not far from where she lived. The price was even lower than what I was paying. I finally gave in and agreed to stay over that Friday night at her place, so we could go and check out this new place together on Saturday.

The room for rent was slightly smaller than my current room. And it was in a big apartment shared with four other girls. One of the roommates, Nancy, was a Ph.D. student at the Film School at NYU. She was the first Chinese student in that school, which was the best of its kind in the US. A fact that she proudly informed us both with. Nancy also came from Beijing. And she told us that the other girls in that apartment all came from some other parts of Asia.

Since all three of us came from the same city, Nancy, Quinn and I went out and had lunch together that day. Nancy had been in NYC for over a year already and had a lot more experience and tips to share with us. She also told me that I could activate my own phone line in my room if I wanted to.

Quinn nudged me again – lower rent, new friend, my own phone number that was not shared with anyone else. Wouldn't that be perfect? Besides, I would be close to her, and I wouldn't need to walk alone for 30-minute in the dark every morning and every night when winter came.

"What else do you want?" she asked.

And I had to agree that all her points sounded like very important factors for me to consider.

So, TWO MONTHS after school started, I moved again. This time, I moved from Brooklyn to Queens. Now that I no longer had to take the train by myself each day, even the commute time became more entertaining and productive. Quinn and I, sometimes with others, discussed school work, shared stories, or even fell asleep on each other's shoulders on our subway rides.

Sometimes Quinn and I would cook and eat our meals together on the weekends, or go shopping for groceries together. There was even an Asian supermarket that we would go on the weekends, to get familiar Asian food. Quinn also tried to teach me a little Tai Chi when we got up early on the weekends, and I showed her how to make dumplings the way Mom and Dad always did.

Days turned into weeks. Winter was coming. Daylight was getting shorter. And time started to go by faster.

I was spending more time in Francesco's lab, as Quinn and Steve did too. Quinn had joined Steve and started working in the "Fish Lab," where they had many beautiful aquarium tanks with different kinds of fish inside. Their lab was located just one story higher in the same building as Francesco's lab, so it was easy for us to visit each other.

Steve had a kind heart. And he was always eager to teach us new things. He was humorous and energetic. He liked to spend time in Francesco's lab too, where two other senior graduate students, Matt and Jason, also worked at.

In this lab and with this group of new friends, I found my new "lab family." People there were very kind, super smart, down to earth, and a lot of fun to be with. I enjoyed my time there, learned a bunch from them, and also learned a little more about them.

WHEN I WAS little, Dad told me that we Chinese had a long history and had gone through five-thousand years of evolution. And that we were "... smarter than the foreigners." he said. And I believed him. He studied overseas for part of his college and graduate school. And he was one of the smartest people I'd had ever known. So, he must knew what he was talking about, right?

But my new friends changed my belief. I was impressed by how smart some of them were, especially Francesco. Often, he seemed to know exactly what I was thinking even though I could still hardly express myself well enough in English. Sometimes when I felt stuck in my attempt to communicate, he somehow would understand what I meant. Sometimes he could figure out the problem by which I was tripped up. He helped and taught me quite a lot, much more beyond the genetics discussion classes.

Sometimes when Quinn and I talked with each other in Chinese, Francesco, or even Steve, would watch us and jump in. They amazed us with how they had figured out what we were talking about, because they usually were right on point as well.

In more than one of the letters I wrote home, I told Dad about my new friends and explained "You were wrong with the *smartness-theory.*" I wrote, "I have found some foreigners who are smarter than many smart Chinese people I know."

Matt was a few years older than most of us, and he acted like a big brother too. He seemed to always want to take care of us, ever so patient and kind. Steve was the spirited and funny one. He was easily excited, and quite animated in how he expressed himself. And Jason seemed to have a special ability in detecting fun and excitement. He often appeared out of nowhere whenever a crowd was forming, adding fuel to the fire.

So when Steve and Francesco got together, there was inevitably loud laughter, with Jason popping up right on cue. It was always so infectious that made Quinn and I just want to laugh with them too, even when we didn't fully understand what they were laughing about. And Matt would watch from a little distance away, while working at his lab bench, and smile his kind and knowing smile.

Sometimes Quinn and I would go to the loft - the Graduate Student Lounge - and join others there, mostly Chinese students, for lunch. It was not just lunch that we shared together. We shared stories, notes, experiences, and observations.

One day, the topic of how people greeted each other came up.

"Did you see Paul?" Paul was another Chinese student who came a year ahead of us.

"What about Paul?" I asked.

"He acts like he is an American. No longer like a Chinese."

"What do you mean?" I was curious now.

"The other day, I saw him hugging this American girl from his class. Like, a *real* hug."

"Wow!"

Wow indeed!

We Chinese don't hug. Not even in the family. Unless you count parents hugging or holding their little kids. Or between people in love, and even that, they shall only do it in private.

Confucianism taught us, since two-thousand years ago, that 男女授受不亲, which meant that men and women shall not touch in the flesh unless they were in the same family. Even when most other traditions were thrown out of the window during the Cultural Revolution, this "rule" probably only got stronger and stricter.

Sure, we shook hands with others, regardless of which sex they were, when needed. But that was all, not more.

"So, how could Paul just disregard this tradition that we Chinese observed for thousands of years?"

"How dare he?"

"Does he not consider himself a Chinese anymore?"

"Sure we are here now in the US. And people, even strangers, hug each other. But that doesn't mean we should do it too. Or... Does it?"

I listened to the lively discussions, wasn't sure if I knew what the "right" answer was. I shook my head lightly. "Maybe one day, if we stayed here long enough, we would also be following the American customs like this?" I didn't know the answer and didn't want to ponder on this any longer, not just yet.

As for the actual lunch itself, I always brought my "budget meal" - bologna ketchup sandwich. Most of the other Chinese students brought their own delicious Chinese dishes. And the American students often bought food from nearby shops.

My Chinese friends laughed at my lunch, saying that I got Americanized too quickly. Though my American friends would pinch their noses and called my lunch "junk-food." And they said that it was super weird for me to put ketchup on a bologna sandwich. I didn't really care either way, my belly was not empty and that was enough for me.

Sometimes other students would join us at the lounge too. And whenever Steve came, he seemed to always ask the same question,

"Hey HE," he asked one of the Chinese students. "Why is it that your last name spelled H-E, but pronounced 'her'?" Steve would ask.

And HE would turn red in the face, and respond in his usual manner with a puff of air, "Just call me Rich!" He would reply each time. And the group would laugh again, watching this episode repeating itself.

Though regardless of how people picked on my lunch choice, my bank account was growing steadily right on schedule.

I had already given back the one thousand dollars that Wendy lent me. And wrote to my friend Chengyun in China that I would be able to repay him $2000 (the amount that we agreed on in exchange for the 12,000 RMB that I borrowed from him), before year-end. That was the last bit of the debt that I had incurred. And it would be amazing when it was cleared.

Chengyun responded in his letter two weeks later. He said that since I was a "poor student," and that his business was doing just fine even without that $2000, he did not want me to return his money for another two years. He also insisted that he did not want any interest payments. As he was just helping me out as "any friend would do."

I told my parents about what Chengyun had said in my next letter home, and how grateful I was for having such wonderful friends like him. Since Chengyun also mentioned that he would be getting married early next year, I decided that I would return his money by the time of his wedding. And, in lieu of paying him any interest, I would give his bride some really nice, expensive, American-made items. Things that might not be available in China, as my wedding gifts to them.

Other things were progressing as well. *Gege* was going to apply for his visa again soon. Even though he had been rejected twice now. He was not giving up on his goal of coming to the US. I told him that now I was in the US, we would definitely be able to get him here soon. He was optimistic, as he had recently been offered an admission with a higher scholarship amount from a university in Chicago. He was hoping to get his visa and come in the spring. I told Mom, Dad, and *Gege*, that now that I was rich, I would buy the airline ticket for him, and I would send him a couple of thousand dollars when he got here as well. That way he wouldn't have to scramble and borrow money from others like I did.

My life was getting more on track. Though most of my classes were still challenging, especially biochemistry and microbiology. The vocabulary was still a big hurdle that I faced for both classes. And I continued to bring my heavy biology dictionary each day. It was used so much that some pages were ready to fall out. But I was thankful for all the help I got in between those covers.

ONE FRIDAY AFTERNOON, the usual group gathered again in Francesco's lab. Everyone was there – Steve, Quinn, Francesco, Jason, Matt and me. The large room was filled with lively discussions and busy activities. Few of us were sitting around the large study desk, reading and talking. Matt was working at his bench again, doing his experiments.

Quinn asked Steve some questions about the fish that they were working on for their research project. Questions on how many baby fish they could expect, to how soon would the baby fish hatch, to how long the eggs stayed around, and how the eggs were fertilized, etc.

Francesco and Steve seemed to be having a lot of fun talking about this topic somehow. I tried to follow their discussion when a word emerged that surprised me in this context, "peanuts?"

"How are peanuts related to this topic of fertilizing fish eggs? Do they feed the fish peanut powder? And does that have an effect on the eggs?" I was quite puzzled.

Steve and Francesco noticed my confusion. And it was as if a light bulb went on in Francesco's eyes. He realized something. He knew what the problem I was having and the answer to it. And he jumped up quickly. Then, half a heartbeat later, Steve realized what was happening as well, and suddenly got really excited too. Even Jason, from across the room, as if his "fun-radar" just picked up some signal and became activated by the excitement. He came running close, refused to be left out on whatever that was happening here.

Francesco practically flung himself onto the large desk in between us. Arm stretched, he snatch my dictionary from under my hand. Flipping it frantically to find the right page, he looked for the word that he wanted to educate me on.

Steve, sitting next to Francesco and across from me, took his direct and animated approach, he raised his elbows with his hands pointing downwards from the sides of his cheeks, forming a big Y. And he moved his arms up and down, while pointing and yelling "Peanuts. Peanuts." at the same time.

Jason stood at the end of our table, looking back and forth between them and me, wheels spinning in his head, as he tried to make sure that he would get the answer to the big secret before I did.

It was becoming such a big commotion within a split second, with Francesco and Steve both wanting to be the first to illuminate me with the big new concept. The air seemed to be charged with their energy, and ready to burst.

"What's going on? Why are they so eager and excited?" I was even more confused now and started to get a bad feeling about this somehow.

"What are they trying to teach me? What word is it that Francesco is going to show me in my dictionary? And why is Steve repeating the word 'peanuts' while pointing downwards?"

Quinn came over as well. She saw my perplexed face and looked at the guys. And she realized what was happening. She knew me better and somehow knew this would not turn out well. She started to warn the boys, and tried to calm them down, while looking back at me with a great deal of concern.

And that was when it suddenly hit me on what they were trying to enlighten me on. That they were telling me it was not "peanuts" that they were talking about. Instead, they were referring to the part of the boy's anatomy that sounded like "peanuts" to me.

Instinctively my face flushed. I was enraged suddenly, for some reason that was unknown even to myself. I jumped up so quickly that I knocked over my chair but I didn't care. I turned around and ran for the door. I saw the realization dawning on Jason's face, and the startled look from Matt. Though I didn't give a damn to what anyone was thinking at this point. I just wanted to get away from that place.

I had no idea why I was so angry. Where that rage came from. Who or what I was angry with. But in my head, I called them names in my native tongue, "流氓! (Perverts!)"

I ran aimlessly in the hallway, didn't know where I was headed or what I was looking for. Until I found a staircase in between two buildings, with a large window left open. The cold winter air that was rushing into the heated hallway felt wonderfully cool against my burning face.

In that hallway, I stopped. And I stayed there for a very long time. I welcomed the crisp blast from outside, and waited for that strange emotion to subside.

I realized that in all my years growing up in China, I had never heard any mentioning of such topic publicly (or privately, for that matter). Except for one special 45-minute class, when all the girls were shown a movie about girl's anatomy, while all the boys were in a different classroom, watching their own version of it. That was our once-in-a-lifetime sex-education, with just enough information for us to understand a little bit about our own bodies, and nothing more.

Outside of that one class, neither in the schools, nor in our family, had the topic of sex ever brought up. Any word related to the topic were to be avoided at all possible costs. And that, was just the way it was.

I had no idea how any other culture dealt with this topic. Nor did I have any idea how the Americans dealt with it. And from what had just happened in that lab, there obviously was a giant gap between the ways how Americans and Chinese handled this topic.

Much later, I decided that it was time for me to go back, no matter how much I wished that I didn't have to face them again. I wasn't sure whether I was still upset with them, or was I too embarrassed for my own irrational behavior. But I was pretty sure that they had no idea how their actions could have triggered such a strong reaction from me.

As I walked in, people stopped talking and got busy with their work. I avoided eye contact with anyone in the room, simply headed straight for the study table. Nobody was sitting there anymore. I sat down on the chair that someone had straightened up for me, buried down my head in front of my book, and tried to read it.

My dictionary was back where I had it, closed neatly and sat next to my opened notebook. Steve and Quinn were gone, probably back to their own lab. Quinn left me a note asking me to call her. I waited on that. It took a long time before someone started talking again in the quiet lab, asking innocent questions in hushed voices.

I felt bad for my friends, for they had to experience my sudden and strong reaction. For something that they did not expect nor understand, something that I didn't quite understand myself. I felt bad that they had to face this unknown and probably unreasonable rage that suddenly filled me earlier, when they did not mean any offense at all. And all they wanted to do was to teach me something new.

And I realized at that moment that the culture shock that I had experienced so far in NYC was nowhere close to an end.

I didn't know why. But the disturbance of that moment in the lab was like a huge earthquake, shaken up yet another part of the culture value and foundation that was built inside of me since the beginning. Value and belief that were embedded and never questioned, deep in my core, until this moment, in this new world called the USA.

EVERY ONCE IN a while, usually the Friday after we received our monthly paycheck, Quinn and I would not bring our usual lunch to school, and we would treat ourselves with a purchased meal instead. The lure of all the delicious food that the "foreign guys" always ate would win at times like this, and we would indulge ourselves with such a special feast.

Sometimes when McDonald's had their specials with two Big Macs for two dollars, we would get a few each, and ate them for lunch, dinner and maybe even the next day.

There was also this fantastic pizza place across the street that filled half of the block with their delicious cooking smell all day long. A place that Francesco and Steve often visited. They would typically get a thin piece of pizza each, with sliced sausages on them (the "pepperoni pizza"). And they would eat them in the lab, holding the steaming pie right in front of us with their bare hands, with orange colored oil dripping down. They would eat with such enthusiasm that sometimes made me just want to smack their faces with those hot pizza slices.

So Quinn and I would get our revenge, on those special days when we felt "rich" and ready to splurge. We would get the thickest slice of pizza in their store, loaded heavy with all kinds of yummy toppings. And we would bring them back to the lab to consume too. Even though it would cost us $3.25 apiece (while the pepperoni slice was at $1.75 each).

At those times, Steve and Francesco would not hide their surprises, maybe even a little bit of envy. With their mouths open, they would watch us as we cut up our slices into small bite-sized pieces, and savor the flavor happily with each bite. And we would both devour our own entire slice of the delicious treat, no matter how full we felt toward the end. That seemed to greatly surprise the boys. The pizza from this little restaurant was so tasty that I even wrote in long letters telling Faye, Connor and *Gege* about it.

Another food concept that was new to me was the "salad." Growing up in China, the only vegetables that I had eaten raw was tomatoes and cucumbers and such. So even though we ate a lot of green leafy vegetables, we always cooked them first. One day Quinn was excited to inform me that the Americans would eat many different kinds of veggies raw, including many leafy vegetables. "Like a rabbit," she commented, "you've got to try it."

So we went to visit this little salad bar near our building on a Friday afternoon. "They let you take whatever you like," she explained to me, "just take one of these clear plastic containers. And put anything you want in it, yourself."

She took two of the containers and handed one to me.

"Oh, that is the lid," she pointed to the flat flap attached to the side of the container, "you fold it over and it will close on itself."

Quinn seemed to be very pleased with all the new knowledge that she was sharing with me. She had come here for the first time just a few days prior, under the tutorage of someone else.

"They will weigh the finished package, and you pay by the weight." Quinn pointed it out. She showed me what to do, which items to try, and which ones weighted less.

"Take that little cup for the sauce," she pointed at the dressings, "try the white creamy one," she suggested, "it tastes really yummy." And she demonstrated it by filling up the little cup with the ranch dressing.

"And keep the sauce outside, so the package would weigh less."

I followed her instructions and her example. A few minutes later, we left the little salad bar with ravish looking boxes of green leaves, red tomato wedges, white and yellow slices of hard boiled eggs, and white mushrooms.

We took them back to the lab to enjoy. Even though we knew the boys would stare and share some smart observations and comments. We did not really care.

Without realizing it, I was slowly expanding my horizon by experimenting with what America had to offer, in many different areas. And I was discovering new flavors and tastes that I had never had before.

Chapter Thirteen

By mid-November, people around me started to talk about Thanksgiving and their plans for that 4-day weekend. This was another new holiday concept for me. Although the idea of families getting together sounded quite like our 中秋节 (Moon Festival). But instead of our moon cakes, the food that people here talked most about was this special big bird called turkey – another new food item on my list to try.

Most of the graduate students in my circle of friends did not have their families around, so the holiday was really just a nice long weekend for us. I planned to use the time to catch up with my studies, as our final exams were approaching quickly, and the TA work had taken a lot of my time lately. Of course, I also wanted to rest, and write more in my journal and letters.

The lab emptied out rather early that Wednesday afternoon. By the time Quinn and I wrapped up what we were doing, it seemed like we were the last ones left in the entire building.

Long weekends were always quite nice and new to us. As students in China, we had classes Monday-through-Saturday during the school year. Although often it was only half-day on Saturdays. Rarely would we have an extra day for a weekend. While we had summer and winter breaks to relax and be with our families and friends, we usually still had quite a load of homework to do during those breaks, so we couldn't just relax and enjoy the time off completely.

Naturally, it was quite nice to have such long weekends sprinkled in during the school year. To get into the weekend mood for Thanksgiving, I sat down and pulled out my collection of letters I had received over the last few weeks and read them again.

I loved to read what Mom wrote, always a lot of pages, front, and back. She often asked me detailed questions about my days, reminded me to wear enough clothes as the weather continued to get colder, and taught me a new recipe or two for simple yet delicious dishes that she knew I loved. Since I never had the need or opportunity to learn cooking when I was back in China, it was really helpful indeed.

Dad wrote few words each time, always in large, stern strokes, always telling me to work hard, and focus on study. Sometimes he even quoted Chairman Mao's famous words "好好学习，天天向上" (Be serious about learning, and be better each day). And he would translate it himself into English literally as "Good Good Study, Day Day Up!" He urged me to "Stay focused, and do not get distracted." Though distracted by *what*, he never clarified. A few times he repeated that I shall "... get the degree in 7 years!" 7 Years?! I would be 30 by then. That was way too long. I couldn't imagine what it would be like to take so long to just get out of school.

Gege was forever curious. He had a lot of questions about the schools in the US, the American students and teachers, the classes, and about the "American life" in general. He suggested that I "Move closer to the school, to experience how the American students live."

"Yeah right." I thought, dismissing his ignorant advice. "Like I would pay $570 a month to share a studio with someone else, just to be close to campus." Now that I had found places at half of that price, with my own room, I was really glad that I did not sign up for the expensive school dorm when I first came.

I also caught up with my journaling, after skipping it for quite a while, since I had been very busy with school, moving, and everything else. It was nice and quiet in the apartment because most of my roommates went out for the weekend. I also spent some time with Quinn at her place where we cooked and ate meals together.

Westbound

Quinn's landlord, an older couple from Hong Kong, invited us to join them for Thanksgiving dinner at their own nicely decorated apartment. They didn't have kids around and treated us like their own. I tried a few slices of roasted turkey for the first time. Flavored with a sweet and tangy cranberry sauce, it was quite delicious indeed.

Quinn and I also took some pictures that Saturday morning. So we could send them home to show our families the places we lived and how joyful we were now.

And I realized that no matter how busy our schedules remained, our lives were improving. We were happier, more content, and neither of us cried as much anymore.

FINALS WERE COMING soon though, for me and for my students in the genetics class. I was drowning in grading all the homework, as well as preparing and grading tests for my TA sessions. And I struggled to find enough time to study for my own exams.

I started to go to the library more again after that holiday weekend. As the quietness there really helped me to focus better. I realized that this was the very first time in my entire life that I had studied *this* hard.

Not even for the famous "entrance exams" that we had in China, where "Your entire future could be determined." as Mom always emphasized in her attempt to make me take these tests more seriously.

And the first one of those "entrance exams" was for entering middle school, when I was only 11 years old. Since we had just moved back to Beijing from Hefei, less than six months prior to me finishing elementary school, I faced double challenges of being in a new school where I didn't know anyone, and to catch up five years' worth of study with a brand new curriculum. Especially since the syllabus in Beijing were quite different from the ones that we had used in Hefei.

My parents pushed me hard to study and to catch up with my classmates. "This exam would determine which middle school you can get into, so it is *critical*." Mom reiterated it to me, and that "It would pretty much determine which high school you would be able to get into later. And ultimately, the college you may be able to go."

Dad echoed her message. He made time in his busy schedule to tutor me during evenings and our 1-day weekends. Though those sessions often ended when I started to doze off during his lectures, forced him to release me to go play outside.

Still, I studied pretty hard for that exam, despite the snickering from some of my new classmates. They laughed at my stretch goal on applying one of the most prestigious middle schools in the capital city, at my awkwardness in how I dressed, and how poorly I performed in some of the tests initially. But I scored higher than all of them where it counted – the city-wide middle school entrance exam. And I got accepted by the school of my first choice, and got into the boarding program there (for students who lived farther away from the school campus).

Three years later, I managed to get good enough score again at the city-wide high school entrance exam. So I stayed in that school for another three years (China's middle- and high-schools usually were on the same campus, and they were 3 years each in length).

Though once those critical exams were over, I tended to relax and my grades always hovered around the middle of my class. And I was still fairly pleased and satisfied with that.

But I understood that I had to take *gaokao* more seriously. I studied hard in the last few months leading up to it. And it paid off. There were two mock exams that Beijing city administered, to help all of its graduating high school seniors prepare for the actual *gaokao*. I advanced to number fourteenth in my classroom (of fifty students) for the first test (which was the highest rank I had ever got in the 3 years of my high school career). Then I edged up further, for the second mock exam, to the eighth among the three hundred students in our school.

As for the real thing, the actual *gaokao exam*, I did unexpectedly well and ranked among the top forty students among the hundreds of thousands of students in Beijing city. It surprised everyone, and was one of the best gifts that I had ever given to my parents. It made them super proud, and earned me the only biology spot that USTC offered for all applicants in Beijing.

But I knew that was not the *real me*. The *me* that was very comfortable to stay in the middle of the rank. As once again, I fell right into after I entered USTC. I was not too troubled by some B's and occasionally C's. Even a B in my favorite math or physics class did not really bother me.

And I was always quite at ease being invisible and quite relaxed in my studies (at least compared to the top students in my classes). The genetic gifts from my parents helped me to stay afloat among the elite of the city for my middle and high school years, and the elite of the country in my college class. I didn't have to exhaust myself with study and schoolwork too much (again, relatively speaking compared to my peers). I very much enjoyed that lifestyle. And that was the *me* that I was most accustomed to and most agreeable with.

"So, why do I feel the need to study so hard now?" I wondered.

In this country where I came as nobody, probably less than nobody. No one knew me, or truly understood me. And I didn't think anyone really cared what grades I got or how well I understood the lectures.

So then, why *did* I study so hard now, here in the USA?

I didn't have time to mull over this question too much. I just put my head down and studied, worked, and studied some more. I tried different methods, too. I borrowed someone else's notes, and borrowed a recording another student did in class. But eventually I gave up on both. As I had a hard time trying to read their handwritten notes, nor could I understand any more of what the teacher had said from the audio cassette tapes.

And I just kept my practice of pre-studying the textbooks, wrote down all the words that I didn't know and translated them. I tried my best to take any note during the classes, and studied the same chapters after class to see how much more sense I could make out of it. By this time I was on my third notebook already. Page after page was still filled with words that needed translation. Though sometimes I realized that I had already translated many of those same words, several times maybe. Regardless, until I truly remembered and understood them, I just kept writing them down in my notebook and looking them up in my faithful dictionaries.

And when the final exams came, the entire school seemed to be under some kind of spell. One could feel the tension in the air, in the hallways and in the lecture halls. Most students seemed to be walking faster somehow. The student-filled hallways were strangely quieter. Many students sat along the walls right outside of the classroom for their next test, reading and cramming up to the last possible second.

For us, the most notoriously scary exam was for biochemistry. There were stories about student leaving the classroom during the middle of the exam, and pulling the fire alarm in the building to disrupt the test. And that the average grade had been in the mid-twenties for the last several years.

Test days for biochemistry and microbiology were back to back. This was the time to see how well we had learned, and how much we had retained.

The lecture halls were even more packed than usual, with graduate students, as well as undergraduate and pre-med students, all taking the same exam together. About a hundred and fifty students filled the theater-style lecture hall for each of these two tests. Somehow there seemed to be far more students at the tests than the classes, which was something I couldn't understand. Why would someone skip the classes if they were taking the course, and why would they still come and take the exams? And how could they do well in these exams if they didn't even bother to show up during the lectures?

I finally got to see why biochemistry test was so hard. Not only were the test questions difficult themselves, but there were so many of them, page after page for the questions alone. Some questions I had to read a few times before I understood enough to try to answer them.

With many unanswered questions and unsure answers, I was quite disappointed when I ran out of time and had to hand in the test sheets.

Microbiology exam was slightly better, although I still had to guess many of the names of the micro-organisms.

DESPITE THE STRESS from the finals, by this time, I really enjoyed being in school, even if it was just for physical comfort reasons. Winter had arrived in New York City. The weather was getting colder. Days were getting shorter. And it often rained or snowed, which made it quite miserable to be outside. Inside the buildings though, it was always very warm. Many American students would wear only t-shirts, especially in our lab.

Such central heating was another new concept to me, as we didn't have anything like it when I was growing up in China.

And it was especially hard in Hefei, a place with very cold winters and terribly hot and humid summers. Back in the days when I was growing up there, it was not zoned for any kind of climate control measures. In those winters we had to move our coal-burning stove into our bedroom to try to stay warm. The annual setting-up and tearing-down of the long metal chimney from the stove (which led the toxic carbon monoxide gas out of the room so it wouldn't kill us), was one of the events that I really enjoyed as a kid.

It was always a family project. I loved working with everyone together. Even the chores were fun. I liked the activities such as cutting out strips of newspaper and gluing them with rice porridge around the window frames. So we could stop the draft of the cold air from invading our room during those cold winter months.

However, keeping that coal-cake burning all night long in the stove each night was always more of an art than science. If the stove door was cracked open a little too wide or closed a little too tight, we would wake up to a very cold room with frozen teapots sitting on that icy-cold stove in the morning.

Beijing was much better. Most buildings, including our last apartment building and in my high school, there were hot water radiators to deliver heat in the winter. I guess it could be called a form of central heating. It was actually really nice. We could even heat or dry up our snow soaked hat or gloves on that precious radiator real estate too. Even if they were only filled in the coldest months and only for a few hours each day.

So it was unbelievable for me to see that in the buildings at NYU, one could *set* the room temperature to whatever they liked, by simply turning a dial and push a couple of buttons. And the room would stay at that level no matter how hot or cold it was outside.

Though I couldn't understand the logic of why people would set the thermometer colder in the summer and hotter in the winter. It made no sense to me at all. Wouldn't that be a lot of wasted energy? If people liked it at a cool sixty-eight degrees in the hot summer days, why would they need to turn it up to a warmer seventy-two degrees in the winter? And if they prefer seventy-two degrees in the winter, then why would they take it down to sixty-eight degrees in the summer? Why couldn't they just do the opposite and save a lot of energy?

And why was it that the American system had to use Fahrenheit, and not the world-standard Celsius? And pounds and ounces versus grams and kilograms? And inches and feet versus centimeters and meters? Why was it that all these measurements had to be so complicated to convert to each other, versus simple millimeter/centimeter/meter/kilometer, etc., where one could just move the decimal point up and down without a calculator? It seemed to me that the school work and daily living became so much more troublesome and complicated by using these hard to covert measurements alone.

Though some other complicated things turned out to be not as bad. Even though it might have taken me a while to figure out.

Like how the adjacent buildings at NYU were connected inside with one another. We could go from one classroom to another, or to the labs, without going outside, even though some were in different buildings. There were a lot of hallways and staircases that connected these buildings. So, even when it rained or snowed outside, we could stay inside the buildings, all dry, toasty and nice.

But the floors for the buildings did not always line up. We could go from the fourth floor in one building, across an enclosed hallway to the next building, and suddenly on the fifth floor now. Eventually, I learned many short-cuts and hardly ever had to go outside during the school day any more.

Unless we needed to go to the library, or attend a class in a building on a separate street, we almost never have to leave this enormous building block during the day in school.

As a Ph.D. student in our department, in our first year, we had an opportunity to pick three different laboratories to do our research rotations. So we could try different branches of biology before making a final decision on which one we would want to focus, and with which professor we would like to work. While the professors also got a chance to pick their future students at the same time.

For my rotation lab choices, I took Francesco's suggestion and asked his professor for my first rotation. And he accepted me. So now, the lab that we usually gather in was no longer just Matt and Francesco's lab, it became my lab too.

In most mornings, I would go to the lab directly when I first arrived at the school. There I usually shed off my outer layers of heavy coats and put down my red school bag. Sometimes I even leave my dictionary there, while attending my classes. I often came back to the lab in between classes, to work on my research project, do my TA work, or study. In the evenings, I often left school directly from the lab with Quinn.

Some of my research experiments took hours to complete and even made me late for my classes occasionally. And I learned that it was just the nature of these things, and all I could do was to plan my schedule better.

I really enjoyed spending time in that lab. With my friends around, the lab had truly become our hub and a spot for us to gather, study, socialize, and work.

December 24 was another quiet day in school. We had started our winter break. Quinn and I went to our labs as usual still but didn't stay for too long. The school was quite empty. Only Steve, Quinn and I were there, doing some light experiments and reading research articles. When the afternoon rolled around, we decided that we would leave early and locked up behind ourselves.

I had nothing planned for that evening, as Christmas was not celebrated in China. So, I thought maybe I could go to bed early, read a book, or write something in my journal.

But Nancy came knocking on my door late in the afternoon. Nancy was quite pretty and very fashionable. "Maybe it is a 'must-have' for students in the Film School?" I sometimes wondered.

"Do you have plans for tonight?" Nancy asked me.

"No." Though resting sounded pretty good.

"Oh, awesome! Let's go shopping at Macy's."

Shopping?

"But I don't need anything." I told her. And I didn't want to spend any money from my precious savings.

"They have fabulous sales. You can get free stuff too. Just come with me. You don't even have to buy anything." she egged me on.

I got curious. Since the next day would be Christmas, and I had heard about some special decorations in stores for this special occasion. Why not go check them out? I called Quinn to invite her to come along.

"No, I am tired. You go." Quinn responded.

So after a quick dinner, I bundled up against the cold night outside. With my thick scarf, long coat, my favorite winter boots and white beanie hat that I had since my college days in China, I left our apartment together with Nancy.

We took the subway back to Manhattan. Though instead of getting off at the downtown Washington Square Park, we stayed on the subway until we got to midtown 34th Street.

My eyes lit up as soon as we came up to the street level again.

Oh, wow, it was so pretty here. Thousands of Christmas lights outlined the buildings, the trees, and the streets, like nothing I had ever seen before. It felt like someone had dragged all the stars down to earth and arranged them marvelously.

I looked around fervently, feasting on the beautiful sight. The cold air was refreshing on my face. There was a light drizzle mixed with tiny snowflakes which made it felt like there were magic in the air.

Nancy opened her mouth wide, with her tongue sticking out, tried to catch the snow. She laughed out loud when she actually did. I was affected by her joyous mood and tried her trick myself. The teeny icy drops tickled my mouth like fairy-dusts, tasted sweet and cool as if they were enchanted desserts.

We progressed slowly on the street, looked around, and enjoyed the view and the fresh coolness of the evening. I had never experienced Christmas before. And to see so many decorations, so many lights, the beautiful moving displays in the store windows, and to hear the music in the air, it was all so amazing and even a little bit overwhelming.

Nancy pointed here and there to show me many new things and told me some of the traditional Christmas stories. Her steps took on a light, bouncy tone. And I followed suit without even meaning to. I couldn't remember when it was the last time that I had felt this way, light and jubilant as if we were in a fantasy world, where my heart wanted to sing and my body wanted to dance.

We waltzed past the Empire State building, the JCPenney store, and walked into the famous Macy's store. It was enormous. I had never been inside a store that was this spacious. My eyes widened, even though they still couldn't take in all that I wanted to see. There were elevators and escalators inside the store itself. The displays were alluring. And there were so many things on sale. So many shiny pieces of jewelry, watches, sparkling plates, cookware; dazzling and colorful dresses; gigantic pictures of gorgeous ladies with flawless skin and a lot of makeup; and many other things that I had never seen. All in one massive store.

"Hey Li," Nancy called from my side.

As I turned to look, I felt this light spray of perfume hitting my face and my nose. I was shocked by the unexpected coolness of the mist and the sweetness of the flowery aroma. It smelled so pretty.

"It's free!" Nancy exclaimed.

Free? Why? How? And they were just left out on the counters for people to spray themselves with?

I shook my head, there were still so many things I didn't understand in America. We kept walking and browsing. Nancy excitedly examined many sample perfume on the counters. And there were so many of them. She got her hands on just about every sample bottle, and sprayed plenty of them on me too. She tried one perfume on one end of my scarf, and asked me to unfold the other end to try a yet different one.

The sweet, fragrant scents; the soft, warming music; the sparkling lights; the magnificent colors and pictures, all seemed to be in such a wonderful harmony. It was as if we were in a mythical kingdom.

Although it felt like we had only just got there, a couple of hours went by quickly. We checked out many different perfumes, looked at a lot of the shiny stuff, the pretty stuff, the colorful stuff. And Nancy even convinced me to try on some coats. I was nervous as I had no intention to buy anything.

"Wouldn't they get mad if I just try things on without buying them?"

Nancy reassured me that it was okay and lots of people do it. So, I tried them on.

The *me* in the mirror looked so different that I could hardly recognize her. The *me* who I had been all my life, was always in plain clothes. Even quite a few hand-me-downs from *Gege*, which I was always eager to inherit and proud to wear. Growing up in the later part of the Cultural Revolution, pretty much the only colors that almost everyone wore for years were grey, green, blue, and white. Though for the last several years, we started to have jeans and some more brightly colored clothes. And that pink sweater that Daddy got me from Germany had become one of my favorite tops.

So who was this strange girl in the mirror staring back at me?

How can a simple jacket change the look of someone so much? With a fitting cut and a beautiful color, it changed my image more than I thought possible. Is that still *me*? Would I actually look and dress like this one day? I wondered as I peeled off the store clothes hurriedly and put back on my old ones.

We were there for a long time until we heard announcements that the store would be closing soon. And we saw the last shoppers leaving already. The vast store was getting quite empty. Even the staff was briskly getting ready to go home and celebrate Christmas Eve themselves.

Nancy and I reluctantly left Macy's. Still empty handed but we brought all the happiness and the pretty smells with us on our wrists and my scarf. It made me feel giggly and lovely somehow.

I kept laughing with Nancy on our train ride back home, especially since the train was quite empty as it was getting late into the night. I liked the mixed perfume smells from my scarf. Even though to someone else, I probably smelled like a "perfume bomb" exploded right next to me.

NEW YEAR'S EVE was another special treat for me. Several of my friends from college reunited to celebrate it together. We planned to go watch the Big-Ball-Drop tradition at the NYC Time Square for welcoming 1991's arrival.

Drove all the way down from Boston, came my good friend Stacy, and her boyfriend Jonathan, another classmate of ours from USTC who had been studying at Harvard for over a year now. They also brought a friend of his, another graduate student at Harvard. Although not an USTC alumnus, Violet also came from Beijing city. And then there were the four of us who lived in New York: Ray, Shirley, Howard (another classmate of ours at Columbia) and myself.

It was so nice to reunite with these friends from college and to meet Violet from my hometown. As we chatted, it almost felt like we were back on USTC campus. We had many old stories to reminisce about and many new experiences to share with each other.

New York City was unusually crowded that night. The giant Red-White-and-Blue ball hung high in the air like a triple-colored full-moon. The weather was super cold. Despite the chilly temperature, there were a lot of people on the street, especially near Time Square. It got really loud with all the noises people were making. And the street vendors selling plastic stadium horns enthusiastically everywhere, "Two dollars! Two for two dollars!" they yelled loudly and blew on the horns themselves to make sure that everyone could hear them.

We walked around for a while, taking in the festivity and some strange costumes people were wearing. Though by the time when it turned 10 o'clock, the temperature had already dipped below freezing. We were so cold and decided that it was not worth the suffering to wait another two hours in this weather in order to watch the event live. So, we headed back to the warm dorm room in Columbia instead, and watched the ball drop on TV.

SOON AFTER New Year's Day, Quinn and I went to visit Matt and Francesco at their apartment on a weekend. That was my first time visiting where "foreigners" lived. And it was the first apartment that I visited in Manhattan since John's place.

It was a simple yet elegant suite that they shared with each other. Bigger than John's place, it was a lot brighter, and cleaner too. Quinn promised them that we would make dumplings and some other Chinese dishes to share. And they seemed to be excited about our visit.

We taught Francesco and Matt how to make dumplings. Though those lumpy and shapeless dumplings they made really made us laugh. Quinn, a better cook (than me) with actual experience of cooking for others, made additional dishes that we all enjoyed. The afternoon went by quickly. I was delighted that the four pairs of chopsticks that I had brought from China finally got a chance to be used.

At the dinner table, Quinn and I had a good chuckle watching the feeble but persistent attempts of Matt and Francesco in using the chopsticks to pick up those slippery dumplings. Until I showed them my cheating method of stabbing the dumplings, and then picking them up with my chopsticks like a two-pronged fork.

We had such a good time that I wrote in a letter to *Gege* the very next day that I had finally "experienced" where the "foreigners" lived, not too far from our school. And that we taught our friends some new tricks on how to use chopsticks too.

153

Chapter Fourteen

Back at school after New Year's Day, we were all anxious to learn about our finals' grades, especially for biochemistry. And for me, also microbiology.

The result for microbiology came out first. I got a score of 83, which was in line with what I expected. But what really surprised me was that the highest grade in our class was only 85. That really boosted my confidence. "At this rate, I should aim for getting the highest grade myself next time!" I set that goal mentally. It was interesting that when Mom pushed me to get that highest grade, I never really cared. Now that she was half of a world away and only wanted me to be healthy and safe. And I, instead, finally began to have the appetite for becoming the best among my peers.

All my Chinese friends started to regret that they did not take "such an easy class." Although I felt lucky for a different reason. Because none of my friends took the class with me, I had to push myself harder to compete with "just the Americans." Or at least, I had no one else with whom I could commiserate in that class. And it paid off.

But it was a completely different story with biochemistry. One of the hardest classes for all the students, not just us the new students from China. It was a required class for biology majors, so we had no choice but to take it. Since I had done quite poorly in earlier tests and our mid-term, I really needed a boost from this final exam.

Rumor had it that the grades were even worse than that from the previous years. That the average score was lower than twenty points out of one hundred. Though I was not sure if that was true, and hoped that someone just made it up to scare us even more about the whole thing unnecessarily.

There were a couple of senior Chinese graduate students among the army of TAs for the biochemistry class. And they told us the date when the grades would be officially released.

That evening all the first year graduate students gathered in the lounge, waiting anxiously to learn the results. For some strange reason, I felt this grade was somehow also a really important indicator for my future here in the US. That it meant so much more to me than just one grade, for one final exam, in one class.

The group of my fellow first year friends had gathered at one end in the lounge, talking excitedly together. I, on the other hand, wanted some peace and quiet, and found a chair in the far corner at the other end where I could sit alone.

I found myself pensive and my mind pondering on some old questions that I hadn't had time to dwell on.

"Why am I so nervous about this one particular test result? Why have I been studying this hard since I came here?" I contemplated once again.

And out of the blue, the answer came.

I often thought of leaving China and coming to the US was like going through a thick fog. It was as if I had shed everything on the other side, in China, the old world of mine, and came to the US, this new world, completely naked. Like a magic eraser had made me into a blank slate.

I had no history here, no reputation, no parents' help paving my way, and no friends telling me that it would all be okay. I came through that dense fog, all by myself, into this new world. Everything I did before I came here was left behind, nobody cared. And everything I did since I got here, was on *me*, and only *me*.

And everything and anything I did going forward, was leaving a fresh mark in this new world.

It was as if I stepped into a land covered by a thick layer of brand new snow. Where there were no prints, except whatever I was going to make now. It felt like I was given a chance to be born again, no baggage, no history, only opportunities.

Nobody cared what I had done in the past, good or bad. Nobody cared which schools I had attended. What my *gaokao* scores were. What my school grades or rankings were. Or who I knew and who my parents knew. None of that mattered any more.

"The only thing that matters now, the only thing that people here care about, is who *I am*, here and now. What *I* will do. What value *I* can provide them. And what *I* can bring to this world, the America." I realized.

And this test score for biochemistry somehow seemed to symbolize how this new *me* was graded. In this new world, in the USA, by the USA standard, and using the USA measurements.

And maybe that was the reason why I was so nervous. Why I studied so hard. Why this particular grade became so important to me. Because this time, all the hard work was no longer for making my parents proud. It was to make me proud, to be proud of myself.

Any maybe that was the reason I wanted to come to the USA in the first place. Why I had no doubt that I would come. Even though I had no idea what it would be like. Even though I was scared, and terrified at the unknown. I wanted to see what I could accomplish on my own, in a country where everyone had their fair share of opportunities to achieve their own goals and dreams.

"Hey!" Quinn came over. She found me.

"What are you doing sitting here all by yourself?" she asked.

I gave her a weak smile. She was such a good friend, always so caring and so cheerful. I was so blessed to have her as a friend.

"Did you hear?" she lowered her voice.

It must be a juicy secret, I waited.

"They said a Chinese student got the second highest score! In biochemistry! It has never happened before!"

Oh, good for him, or her, I thought. There were some other Chinese students in this class besides the five of us. Even though I didn't know many of them. I guessed that most of them had been in the US for many years or they had grown up here, and that they had no challenge with English as far as I could tell.

"Wow, can you imagine? This class? A Chinese?" Quinn marveled. "Oh, come on. Let's go over there, join them and wait together."

She dragged me up. And we walked over to the other end of the lounge and joined the group.

It was getting late. We ran out of topics to talk about. But still, no grades showed up yet. Nobody wanted to leave though. Everyone was staying and waiting.

The door opened. One of the biochemistry TAs came in and rushed over. In a hushed voice, he announced.

"It's coming, they are bringing the grades out ..."

He looked around us, seemed to be searching for someone. And when he saw me, he stopped. He stared at me and announced,

"You! You did great! You scored the second highest in the entire class!"

Me? I looked around me. He must be talking to someone else. But all the eyes I met were looking back at me. Me? I looked at him again. And he was still staring at me, nodding his head with a big smile on his face.

But there was no way that he meant *me*. Maybe he had mistaken me for someone else? I didn't even know his name. Did he know who I was? Or what my name was? How could he be so sure? How could *I* be the number two in the whole class? This class? The biochemistry class? With all these American students? All these intelligent, beautiful and native English speakers? Graduate and pre-med students? With over a hundred of them who grew up here, speaking this language as their native tongue. How could it be *me*?!

"Yeah, you! Li Tian. You got fifty-two! The average is twenty-seven."

"Fifty-two? Wasn't that a failing score? And that was number two in the whole class? What was the highest grade then?"

My thoughts were swirling like crazy. And then I realized that everyone was looking at me now. Quinn was more excited than if it was herself who did well, jumping around me, and repeating the news to the others. I just stood there, dumbfounded, could not believe it.

"Is this a dream? It must be a mistake. He was wrong. It couldn't be me..."

But he wasn't wrong. And I did get the second highest grade in that class. And a B for the semester for biochemistry. As much as I valued this test score, I didn't expect that it could mean so much to me. My throat got tight. I choked back the tears and squeezed a smile back at Quinn's sunny face.

In my mind, in this new world that called America – me – this new girl who came with nothing, as a "nobody." Who had no history here. And yet, it didn't matter. All that I had to endure and sacrifice had paid off. All the heartbreaks and headaches, the tears and blood, the challenges and loneliness. None of that mattered now. As I had just left my first meaningful mark here. A mark that I could be proud of. A mark that was worth all the suffering and all the hard-work.

As I looked around at the glowing faces of my friends who surrounded me, I suddenly realized that I was not just part of this group. With this grade, I also represented this group – my fellow students from China – in a small way. And it was not just the group of 5 of us, but so many others too, scattered in different departments, schools, and universities across the nation. All of us were fighting so hard to establish our new identity here, build our new reputation, and earn our rightful spots in this country.

No matter how tough the situation and competitions were (I could only imagine the competition my friends faced in Harvard, Columbia, etc.), no matter how different our background were, and no matter how bad were the cultural shocks, we were all working fervently. We all sacrificed so much, even just to be here. We were all so amazing in our own ways. And we would persevere in building our new lives, right here in America.

To me, this grade seemed to have taken on a much deeper meaning because all of this. It had become a small window into the Chinese student community, or even the broader immigrant community as a whole. In my mind, it was an example that we would do whatever it takes to succeed here. And that we should not, would not, and could not be ignored. And the schools across the nation were not wrong in taking on more excellent students, from China and other countries, in the years to come.

And *that* was a mark that I could write home about, to my family, to my teachers, and to my friends.

And to make them all very proud.

Chapter Fifteen

Came February, I had spent my first Chinese New Year away from home, away from China. It was my 本命年 (Benmingnian, the years that share the same Chinese zodiac sign with one's birth year, once every 12 years). Some old wives' tales warned that one could be extra vulnerable to being snatched away by the underworld during such years. So, Mom urged me in her letter to wear something red at all times, to ward off any evil spirit from hurting me, or even taking me to their world. I found a little red string and wrapped it around my wrist.

The weather seemed to be the worst yet in New York City. We had rain and snow, which made some trips down the staircases at the subway station extra slippery and scary. But in Queens, where we lived, the snow-covered ground stayed drier and cleaner, probably because there was much less foot traffic.

Subway rides became a little more interesting when we rushed onto the wrong train without noticing it, and waking up to a completely different final destination. Or when we found talented musicians from some of the top Chinese music schools playing sweet and familiar melodies on the subway platforms, with their instrument cases open at their feet to accept donations. Or when I met the eyes of a complete stranger and felt compelled to actually return their smiles.

Though a more memorable incident happened in late February. Earlier that day, the guys in the lab talked about some subway bombing attack in London, where quite a number of people were hurt. I didn't have a TV or radio, nor did I read newspapers since the time I found my first home. So the guys in the lab were pretty much my only source of news. I wasn't paying much attention to their discussions. But it left an impression on my mind to hear them speculating about what they would do, if there were a subway bombing right here in Manhattan.

That night as I was walking down the stairs at the subway station on my way home, I saw a familiar sight of a homeless person sitting on the dirty and wet stairs. Head bent low, he held a drinking cup with a couple of coins inside. And he was shaking it weakly to plead for money. Somehow at that moment, I remembered the discussion earlier in the lab about the subway bombing. And I thought, "Well, if someone did bomb the NYC subway tonight and it killed me, I wouldn't have much need for this money anymore." So, I stopped in front of the beggar, took out all my change and dropped it into his cup.

The vagrant was startled at the continued dropping of coins. He looked up with surprised and puzzled eyes and thanked me. That night I got home just like most other nights, uneventful. And I felt relieved and grateful for the peace that we had enjoyed.

THE CHINESE NAME for our New Year holiday is called 春节 (Spring Festival). And spring had indeed followed quickly on the heels of that weekend, even though I was no longer in China. It was almost like a fairy-lady had breathed her magic into Washington Square Park. Tiny green baby buds, pink cherry blossom, and white crabapple flowers all appeared beautifully on the bare branches of the trees, seemingly overnight.

The days started to get longer again. The temperature was warming up. By this time, I had completed my first lab rotation at Matt and Francesco's lab, moved on to the second laboratory, and started working for our new department chairman on my second project.

Though whenever I had some chunks of free time, I still went to Matt and Francesco's lab. The friendship in our lab-family was getting stronger, and I continued to learn and enjoy my spare time in that lab.

AS FOR OUR new TA assignments for the spring semester, I had joined my fellow first-year TAs at the Animal Diversity lab sessions for the undergraduate freshmen class. The workload was much heavier. And this time, I was paired up with a handsome and tall American student named Chris.

Chris was also a first-year TA but seemed to have very high confidence about himself and his skills. He was happy to share his suggestions and opinions with me, even when I didn't ask for any. By this time, my English skill and my confidence had improved even more. And I felt ready to teach the class myself, with or without much help from others. So Chris and I agreed that each of us would be in charge of teaching every other week.

For our first week's TA sessions, our job was to direct the students to dissect dead rats. And I was quite thankful that Chris volunteered to take the lead for this class.

As I had never seen rats as huge as these in my entire life.

My goodness. They seemed to be as big as cats. And don't get me wrong, we had plenty of rodents in China too. Especially since I went to boarding schools, I had seen my fair share of rats and mice. Even though we didn't have much food for years, there was always leftover lunch and dinner dumped into a special basin near the sink, in our girls' communal bathrooms. And if we went there when it was quiet, day or night, we would likely find a mouse or a rat enjoying the feast in the basin.

And occasionally, if we weren't careful and left our dorm room door open for too long, one might slip into our room. And it was always quite an exciting team-sport to eliminate the pest. No matter how smart and fast those little creatures were. Somehow, someway, we would find a way to get rid of them. Trust me, when you have a group of six very smart, creative and determined teenage or twenty-ish girls having the same mission, fueled by strong and passionate hatred for pests, miracles could happen.

So those mice and rats in China were very well fed as one could imagine, and pretty fat for their own good. But *none* of them were *this* big as the ones we had for the biology lab sessions at NYU.

We were given a deep bucket of such dead creatures for each of our lab sessions. Before I said anything, Chris enthusiastically volunteered to handle the distribution of those formalin-soaked, pale, cold, smelly, and motionless carcasses to the students. And there were some very eager students who rushed over to grab their share. I, on the other hand, gladly stayed as far of a distance away from that cluster of people as possible. Especially since I thought the student at the far corner of the classroom had a question that needed my attention.

See, the truth was, even though I majored in biology for the past 5 plus years, I really thought that I should have majored in engineering instead. And it was not just because my whole family were engineers. Even if it was for nothing else, I just loathed working with animals, or even fish - anything moved, alive or dead. Cultured cells in a flask, or bacteria in a beaker was okay for me, even fruit flies were tolerable, but anything that was bigger than a fly and could move on their own would fall on my list to be avoided at all possible costs.

Though no matter how disgusted I felt about those rat corpses, I didn't want to portray the image of a TA and graduate student in biology who would stay far away from experimental objects. In my view, TAs were just like any other teachers, we should always set good examples to the students.

Back in the classroom, now that the students had taken their specimens and were given the instructions on what they shall do, all Chris and I had to do was to supervise and address any questions as they came up. Chris came over to me at this point, proudly announced that he had everything handled and that I could just relax.

Seeing that I didn't really respond, as I had no idea what he was expecting me to say, he stuck his hand over and tried to tickle me. I stepped to the side, swatted his hand away, and said sternly, "Don't do that."

"Why?" he asked, seemed to be a little taken aback.

"I don't like it." I told him seriously. I was surprised that he didn't see the improperness here. We were teachers, even though we had the word "assistant" in our title, in these classes, we were the teachers. 为人师表 Means teachers should always set proper behavior and learning examples in front of others, especially to their students.

And how could something like tickling each other be appropriate for teachers to do in front of their class? How could that be a good example?

Plus, Chris and I weren't close enough to act like that even if we weren't in front of a class. In my view, such acts were considered quite intimate and was only appropriate with family members or close friends. Chris and I had just started working together and we barely knew each other.

In any case, apparently that was not the response that Chris was looking for, as the smile on his face disappeared quickly. Turned around, he headed toward the door, and left with "I will be back in five minutes."

Forty minutes later, and just about five minutes before the class was over, Chris came back.

"Did you miss me?" he asked me cheerfully.

Frankly? No. I wasn't pleased with how he acted, but I handled the class just fine during his absence.

So I answered him severely, "No. Why?"

For the second time in that one-hour span, my words wiped the smile away from his face. Chris mumbled something under his breath as he turned and walked away again.

After that, things slowly got better. Chris still left the classroom from time to time, though usually not for very long. I really didn't care either way. As I was able to take care of the class when I was in charge, with or without him. For those sessions that Chris led, I stayed around in the class to help the students when they needed it. As I believed it was my job to be present in all of the sessions, regardless of who was the main TA in charge. And it was a job that I took seriously. So I could earn all the privileges that came with the job - the waived tuition and my $1400 a month stipend - fair and square.

Even though I never had the type of connection and rapport with Chris as I did with Francesco, Matt, Steve, and even Jason. As time went on, we talked more and learned a bit more about each other too. Chris had an outside job bartending not far from the school and made good money from the tips he got there. Though once or twice, as he left the bar late at night, with the cash tips in his pockets, he was almost robbed. Luckily he was a fast runner and was able to escape his attackers.

Chris was the first American student who I knew worked outside of the school to make more money. And hearing those close-call stories of nearly becoming a victim of violent crimes, somehow it helped me to empathize and respect him a little more too.

With these improved understanding and respect, despite the rough start, our collaboration in and outside of the classroom became much more harmonious as time went on.

EARLY SPRING IN NYC sometimes still got cold and felt almost like winter had come back again. But inside our lab, it was always toasty, nice, relaxed and even fun.

A visiting scholar from Korea, Ming-Jun, came and joined us for a short while, to work on a collaboration project in Francesco's lab. Ming-Jun was older than most of us. He was nice and soft-spoken with a strong accent. Although he was probably still a lot better with his English skills than I was when I first came to NYC.

Ming-Jun came into the lab one day and excitedly called us over to show us a picture of his newborn baby son.

Now, I was still not a "kid person." But I joined the little crowd nonetheless, to take a look at this special treat. Although the second I saw that baby's picture, the only thing that came to mind was - "Wow! I have never thought a baby can look like this."

All the babies I had seen up to that point in my life, I realized, were from posters and calendars. And they were all big-eyed, chubby-cheeked and really cute. This unfortunate baby was the opposite. And the only thing came to mind was "This baby does not look very good. Not at all."

So I kept my mouth shut. Since I couldn't think of anything nice and appropriate to say. Jason, as usual, popped up in the crowd again. This time he was in the front and looked at the baby picture up-close. He broke the long silence in the room.

"Ohhhh," he said, "how cute!"

Cute? I didn't think that was the right word to describe *this* baby. But obviously that made Ming-Jun very happy. He smiled from ear to ear, and was so very proud. I didn't know what to say. Feeling a little bewildered, I pulled my gaze away from the picture, just to look straight into Francesco's bemused eyes.

We shared the same look. So the second our eyes met, laughter threatened to burst out from both of us. We hurriedly turned around to separate ourselves from that little crowd and the proud daddy, while trying to hold our laughs in and not bring any attention from others. When "Owww!" an elbow poked me sharply in my ribs. I looked back, Quinn was right behind me, with a big smile on her own face. She was pulling away as well, trying to hold back her own laugh that was about to bust out.

THE DAYS KEPT growing longer and the spring, getting deeper. By this time, Quinn and I were often joined by another first-year Chinese student, Daisy, to take our daily commuting train ride between home and the school.

Daisy was a slight girl. Even though I was quite petite myself, I always felt that she was so much lighter. And I worried that she could be blown away if the wind just picked up a couple of notches.

One evening as we were leaving school, and walking through Washington Square Park to go to the subway station, something unusual happened.

It was a colder spring day. The sun had already set. The daytime crowd had already left and the park was getting pretty quiet. In the dusk, the light breeze from earlier was turning stronger into a freezing gust. We walked against the wind with our heads lowered. I pulled my wool scarf higher to cover up my chin. No one was talking. We were saving whatever topic we had in mind for the train ride, where it would be warm and more relaxed. When suddenly –

"WHERE'S THE MONEY?!"

Out of nowhere, a person jumped right in front of us. With his arm stretched out, he had blocked our way forward. I was startled. We all stopped dead in our tracks. I looked up from the ground. A homeless guy, with a dirty hat and a tattered jacket, the original color of which was hard to tell. His blue eyes were looking at us. And he was asking, no, *demanding*, for money.

But somehow his face was not one of menace or even threat. It was almost expressionless, as if he was just checking in to see how our day was.

At the corner of my eye, I saw a silhouette of a policeman less than a block away. He simply stood there, motionless. It was a little hard to tell in the dimming light, but it seemed to me like he was facing in our direction.

Somehow the image of that far-away policeman and the lack of violent expression on our attacker's face gave me the courage to blurt it out, in a louder voice than his,

"Yeah! Where's the money? I want money too!"

The guy was surprised by my response. His eyes widened and he stared at me. I met his gaze square on. After pausing for a second, he blinked. Then he became visibly relaxed and retreated to one side, while murmuring,

"That makes sense." As he turned and walked away.

A couple of seconds later, we un-froze ourselves and continued on with our short trip to the subway station.

After we boarded the train, Daisy finally found her voice. She asked shakily, "What happened back there in the park?"

"Nothing, he just wanted to tease us." I told her, while my heart rate started to calm down itself.

THE TAIL-END of the winter got super chilly. And it brought some major disappointing news to me. I finally got a response back from Connor's school, informing me about their decision on rejecting my transfer request.

I was devastated.

That night on the phone with Connor we both cried. Connor was so distraught that he sounded as if we would never see each other again. I told him that I would not give up and would continue to apply. I would apply to more professors, departments, and even to other schools in Los Angeles too. And that I was determined to do whatever I could to be there with him soon.

THOUGH NO COLD spells could stop the steps of the spring. Pretty soon, the lawn in Washington Square Park turned to a lush and vibrant green, and the flowers started their annual bloom. Beautiful and brightly colored, the park looked dazzling and smelled fragrant.

With the warmth of the sunlight, we were able to shed off those thicker coats and heavier boots that weighted us down in the past few months. It was so wonderful and light that I felt like I could almost fly.

On one such sunny afternoon, Quinn and I got a chance to take a short walk through the park. We thoroughly enjoyed the fresh air and the pretty sight in the sun, and felt rejuvenated as we headed back to our next class. Near our building entrance, Quinn noticed that someone was handing out some small items to the students passing him by.

That was another thing that amazed me here in the US. People would give you free stuff, right on the street, to complete strangers and even thank *you* for accepting them. We never had that in China. It was simply unheard of. "Why would anyone spend money to get something, just to give it away to strangers?"

"Oh, they are candies, take one!" Quinn nudged me. Taking one for herself, she made sure that I got one as well. I took it offhandedly from the guy. Somehow earned a bit of a surprised and inquisitive look from him. But I didn't give it any thought.

The package was round and small like a lollipop, though without any stick. It was quite flat, not at all hard like a regular candy. And it was wrapped in a small plastic baggie with some tiny pictures. I held it between my thumb and index finger without paying it much attention, planned to save it for later when I got hungry. We walked into the building with a few others. I continued to tell Quinn about my research project. On what I planned to do next, and how that could help me to learn new things and even possibly lead to some new and exciting discoveries.

We stepped inside the elevator with some other students who were also going upstairs. While I continued on talking, Quinn started to unwrap her candy. Then I noticed that she was distracted by her candy and was no longer listening to me anymore.

"What's wrong?" I asked her.

And I felt the attention from a couple of American guys in the elevator on Quinn as well. They seemed to be watching her as she continued to unwrap the candy in her hands, with an amused or even incredulous look on their faces. I watched her as she stopped pulling the candy out of its wrapper halfway. Hesitating, she flipped the package around to inspect it closely.

And suddenly, "Ewwww," she squeaked. And she quickly fisted the candy and its wrapper and stuffed them into her coat pocket. "扔掉！扔掉！" (Drop it! Drop it!) She urged me in Chinese in a hushed voice. Though she wasn't even looking at me. In fact, she acted as if nothing had happened.

I was surprised and confused. So I didn't do anything. Noticing that, Quinn pulled her hand out of her pocket, grabbed the candy out of my hand literally, and stuffed it into her pocket as well.

While the American guys who had been watching her started whispering and chortling among themselves, I was totally puzzled by what had just happened.

"What is it? What's wrong?" I asked her.

Why did she want to throw away our candies? Why did she take away *my* candy? Were they bad candies? Or bad wrappers? Were they not candies?

Seeing my irritated and bewildered face, Quinn tried to explain to me. "They are not candies. They are for that thing that you don't like to talk about."

Hmmm? What thing? What was it that I didn't like to talk about? I was even more confused now.

"The thing that sounded like 'peanuts'...." She was forced to give me more hints, though there was a twinkling smile in her eyes now.

Oh my goodness! The scene from a few weeks ago in the lab flushed back into my mind. "Ewwww!" this time it was my turn to squeal, "Why did you tell me to take one?"

I blamed her. The other guys in the elevator who were still watching us started to laugh aloud. So was Quinn. And I found that I was infected by their laughter and started to giggle myself. I wiped my fingers on Quinn's jacket. It was my attempt to get rid of the residuals from that little parcel, and to punish her for putting me through such a humiliating episode.

And in that lighthearted laugh, I suddenly realized that the cultural foundation that had come to this country with me, deep inside of my core, had been broken down even more.

Without me noticing it, little by little, brick by brick, the old custom of rigidness, secrecy, and suppression was being replaced quietly by a sense of liberty, openness and more acceptance. Right here in New York City, in the heart of the melting pot of the USA.

Chapter Sixteen

Spring was showing off its full glory. And the weather was getting nice and warm. Summer was following quickly behind. With the end of the school year quickly approaching, a lot of people started to talk about their summer plans.

I thought about finding a waitressing job in a Chinese restaurant to make more money, as a chance to experience working outside of the school. But I also wanted to go to LA to see Connor and my friend Faye.

Earlier in the school year, I picked up an advertisement flyer from American Express in our classroom. It stated that we could get vouchers for low-cost, round-trip airline tickets anywhere within the continental US. We simply needed to apply for their credit card and using it. What a remarkable deal. I applied right away. The card came in the mail pretty quickly. I had used it for some necessities, and had indeed received a voucher for a round-trip airline ticket at the price of $118. All I had to do was to call the airline and book a flight, anywhere I wanted to go.

Well, I really wanted to go to LA, to see Connor and Faye. Faye knew Connor as well. I had shared with her more about my life in NYC than probably anyone else. I had told her about my pain and joy, my learning in NYU, my new friends there, the pizza from that little Italian shop near school, and so much more. I'd also learned about many things that she had experienced in LA. She seemed to have adapted quite nicely there.

"Come to LA," she enticed me, "we can have a lot of fun together."

Yeah, that could be good.

And Faye had listed many other good points about LA to persuade me. People were nice and relaxed. The schools were great. The weather was unbelievable. And she had even bought a car.

"And it is closer to China too," she reminded me. "So, when we can go home to visit, it wouldn't be as far, or as long of a flight, as from New York." She even pulled this card out as I had shared with her my ordeal while traveling to NYC.

But I had not heard any good news from the professors, departments, or schools to whom I had sent my second and a much larger wave of transfer requests. I had written to quite a few professors, in both universities where Connor and Faye attended, but had yet to hear any positive response.

"And if I can't get an offer, there is no way I can afford to leave NY for LA. Then what should I do for the summer? Staying in NY and work to make more money, or go to LA to see Connor and Faye and try the transfer from there?" I debated back and forth, but could not decide.

Though shortly thereafter, a phone call made that decision for me.

A call with Connor.

Looking back, I realized that over the past couple of months, especially since I was rejected by Connor's school for my initial transfer request, my calls with Connor had changed in some subtle ways. It often frustrated me when he did not pick up the phone at the time as we planned to talk, or he didn't call when he said he would. The reasons were often that his work went longer, or he had to spend extra time in the class, or that he went to play ball with his friends and forgot to keep track of time.

Since NY was three hours ahead of LA, it meant that I either went to bed worried about something bad might have happened to him, or I had to stay up late trying to reach him or waiting for his call, often deep into the night.

By this time, we talked less frequently too. And sometimes we even skipped a week or two here and there.

And it was not because of my budget concerns anymore. By this time, I had already fulfilled all my promises. I had purchased a ticket for *Gege* to fly to Chicago, and helped him get started there back in March by making sure he had a place to stay and sent him a $2000 check. I had also paid back Chengyun his $2000, and had gotten his bride a very nice package of expensive American wedding gift items. Almost everything in that package was purchased from that giant Macy's store, with several bottles of famous perfumes that Nancy recommended in it too.

It felt great to be completely out of debt, helped *Gege* to stay out of it altogether, and had a few months' worth of living expenses in my bank account. Though saving money was still very important to me. As a higher balance in my bank account gave me the feeling of more peace of mind and financial security. But the heavy financial burden that I had felt when I first came to the US had certainly lessened enormously.

And I surely did not mind spending money, or time, on things that were important to me. Things like staying better connected with Connor. But lately, during our calls, he seemed to be often distracted. And I felt that we were not always on the same page as before. Connor's life and experience in LA seemed to be quite different from mine in NYC. It was remarkable to see how two cities and universities in the same country could provide such disparate experiences.

It sounded like everything was rosier about Connor's life in LA, except trivial things like when he complained about this girl in his class. She seemed to be very pretty but somehow always gave him a hard time for some reason. And it really bothered him that she treated him that way. When he tried to argue back, she would be so hurt that she even cried in front of others, which made him feel confused and guilty in return.

But even though he talked about her quite a bit, "You have nothing to worry about." Connor told me. "She has a boyfriend and I have you." he said.

Which actually baffled me a little bit. Why would I worry? And what should I worry about? But I didn't say anything and didn't give it too much thought either.

Quinn didn't seem to like Connor all that much. Even though she had never met him, and she had only learned a little bit about him from what I had shared with her on our subway rides. When I told her the stories about this pretty girl, and that I didn't understand why Connor would tell me not to worry. Quinn seemed to think that maybe I should be more concerned.

"He's changing his heart." she commented. "You should forget about him. There are so many great guys here."

I did not respond. But in my head, I dismissed her input. "No, you don't know us. Connor and I love each other. And we will get married someday after we get back together." I thought.

Or at least in my heart, I believed that was the plan.

We had been together for about four years now, even though not in the same city for the last several months. He was the first and only guy I had ever loved. And he had even given me a "promise ring" before he left Beijing.

And that was when the call that changed everything for me happened, on a Friday night in late May. By this time, I had already finished all my finals, and was just wrapping up the last lab rotation and waiting for my grades.

On that call, I told Connor that I was considering to come to LA to see him sometime during the summer break. But instead of being very happy and excited about the news, as I was expecting, he responded by saying that he didn't think that was necessary. I was astounded and confused by his reply. And that was when he proceeded to tell me that he had fallen in love with this new pretty girl and that she loved him, too.

"Oh, how blind and silly!" I thought. "You are just lonely. You don't love her. You just want to have someone there to be with you."

We had been together for so long. What we had was true love, and that would never change. It was only because we were too far apart and we hadn't seen each other for way too long, that he thought he loved someone else. Because she was right there, and spending time together made him believe that he loved her. But that was not real love.

"I just need to be there. And you will see what we have is true love." I was convinced.

Though on the phone, I didn't say all that much. Connor seemed to have made up his mind, and I wasn't able to convince him otherwise.

"You are free!" he declared. Even after I tried to persuade him not to give up on us. I stopped fighting with him on the phone after a while. "I just need to go show him," I decided in my mind, and "for him to see it for himself."

It was well past midnight when we finally hung up the phone. And I opened my journal and poured everything into it. I wrote and cried, cried and wrote. Hours went by. Tears smudged the words and the pages. And I did not stop. I kept on writing. I wrote all the things that I wanted to say on the phone but didn't. All the reasons that I believed our love was worth saving. That I understood how lonely he must have been and why he felt this way toward this new pretty girl. I forgave him for all that he had done. I believed that I just needed to be there so he could make the best choice for himself. And there was no doubt in my mind that the right choice would be me.

I wrote through that long dark night until the sun came up, until I ran out of pages in my journal and ran out of tears in my eyes.

A couple of hours later, I made a call to United Airlines and used my voucher for the earliest flight available for LA, in four days' time.

There were a lot of things that I needed to finish and wrap up at NYU before I was ready to leave. And I needed to prepare for the possibility that I may not come back to NY, or the possibility that I would be back before the school started again.

Everything was up in the air.

The only thing that was crystal clear to me was that I needed to go to LA. I needed to go see Connor as soon as possible, and to do whatever I could to save our relationship.

Quinn believed that I was making a big mistake, when I told her that afternoon about what had happened and about my plan. She tried to convince me not to go, that Connor was not worthy or deserving of my love.

But nothing, and nobody, could have changed my mind and my belief at that point.

The decision was already made. I just needed to finish whatever I had to do at school and at home, take this trip, and go to LA.

On the last day at NYU, when I said goodbye to my friends, I hugged them. I didn't even think about it or debate whether I was abandoning my Chinese heritage and culture. It just felt right and appropriate.

For the last nine months, these people had become my family, my only family in this new world. They taught me so much, and helped me in so many ways and so deeply. I was so grateful for them, more than they could ever know.

Somewhere deep inside I almost felt like I was betraying them, because I didn't tell them clearly about the possibility that I might not come back after the summer. I was not sure what would happen in LA myself. But that guilt nagged me deep inside, as I thanked them from the bottom of my heart, and promised them that I would call and write.

It was true that I had no offer yet from any school or any professor in Los Angeles for a possible transfer. And I had two offers, from the three professors with whom I had done my research rotations. Offers for me to stay as their own Ph.D. student. Both professors were successful, nice, intelligent, and well respected. Both would be great advisors for me.

But this city of New York, and this school of NYU, also brought me so much pain in the beginning, so much headache and heartache. That a part of me would be relieved to escape all of that, maybe even forget some of it.

While Los Angeles, if it was indeed as promising as Faye wanted me to believe, it could be a nice change. And no matter what was waiting for me there with Connor, it could also mean another new beginning. Another adventure for me to shed the good and the bad of my past. A chance to build another version of me, on the foundation of this much more confident and capable self.

CHAPTER SEVENTEEN

May 1991

FOR THE SECOND TIME IN MY LIFE, IN LESS THAN TEN MONTHS' span, I arrived at an airport and got on an airplane. This time, I only brought with me my small suitcase and my big red canvas messenger bag.

Earlier that day, I canceled my own phone line, and said goodbye to Nancy. With that, I left my rental room, the place that had been my home for the last seven months.

Also for the second time since I came to the USA, I left my two large suitcases behind, at Quinn's place this time. Saying goodbye to Quinn was the hardest thing to do. As she had become a sister that I wished I had and the most important person in my life in NYC. I owed her so much but I was now leaving her behind.

"If I come back to New York City, I will find a new place close to you and get my bags then." I told Quinn, "But if I somehow end up staying in Los Angeles, I will call you and let you know. And we will find a way to get the suitcases shipped there."

The future was unknown.

But compared to that young, innocent, naive, ignorant, scared, and lost girl, who came to this country all by herself, just nine months ago, I was buttressed by my experience in New York City. And I felt like I had become a completely different person.

It was a strange and quiet revelation. But I knew now in my heart that no matter what happened next, I would be fine.

And whatever was waiting for me in LA, it could never be as bad as what I had faced when I first arrived in NYC. Because now *I* was better, stronger, and so much more capable and confident.

"Please buckle your seatbelts for the final descent into the Los Angeles International Airport." our flight captain announced.

I looked through the small oval window. From high above, I saw a sprawling city covered by a light grey fog. The buildings, not as tall nor crowded together like the ones in Manhattan, looked as if they were shifting in that fog.

And I saw, although not very clearly, the wide roads with lanes of cars, like giant snakes moving, that must be the "freeway" that I had heard so much about from Faye and Connor. They told me that I would need to buy my own car, and learn to drive, if I moved here.

"More adventures ahead." I thought.

"That is not fog."

I was startled by the comment from my next seat neighbor. He looked at me, seemed to know exactly what I was thinking.

"It is smog," he explained further, "not fog. It's pollution."

Well, whatever it was, we descended below it and landed safely. Though gripping tight at the armrests of my seat, as we went through the slight turbulence in the air, I did not throw up on this flight.

"Even my stomach is getting tougher." I thought happily with a hand on my abdomen, and a satisfied smile to myself.

We were then on the ground, on the other side of that fog, or smog.

"Welcome to Los Angeles. Enjoy your stay." The captain gave his final words, as he parked the plane in front of our gate, and cut off the engine and the intercom.

With no idea what would be waiting for me here, but fearless and determined in my heart, I announced to the universe, "Here I come, Los Angeles …"

Acknowledgment

On President's Day February 2019, my 17-year-old daughter and I dropped off my son back at his college, and headed back home from Los Angeles.

We talked about ideas for possible video projects that she might want to do with her friends at school. She was considering making a video that had more significant meaning to it. And that was when she asked me, out of the blue,

"Mom, can we re-enact your journey coming to the US from China?"

I almost choked up by her question. As I am certain for any mom, to have a teenage daughter putting forward a request like this would touch her heart.

As for me, I have always seen so much of myself in her. Both of us are the youngest in our families. Both of us have loving parents and a wonderful, smart, and perfect *Gege* who we absolutely love and admire.

Though we are quite different too. She is the most strikingly beautiful girl in the world, while I am not. She is talented with her language skills and emotional intelligence. And I have always been biased toward math, physics, and logical thinking.

Though even if I trust that she remembers many of the stories I have shared with her over the years, I did not think that was anywhere close to enough material to base a video project on, no matter how short it might be.

So I decided that I would write the stories down for her.

And I knew nothing about writing a screenplay. Just as I knew nothing about how to write a memoir.

But when I sat down that Monday night and started to type, the words just poured out of me as if a floodgate had opened. I wrote more each night that week. And by midnight that Friday, I finished a book, my first manuscript. The first version of this book.

As I wrote, especially toward the end of that week, a different purpose started to surface. An overwhelming feeling came over me – everyone has a story like this. And if, by bearing my soul naked as it was written here, if this book can inspire another person or two, to write out his or her own journey, even if it might be just for themselves, or for their loved ones, then publishing this effort might be worth it.

And that was how this book, *Westbound,* was born.

I want to thank all the people who were part of my journey during that special period of time covered in this book. And I want to thank all the people who have been part of my life's journey up to now from the very beginning. Life has continued to teach me great lessons, and one of the most important ones is – people in our lives matter, things don't.

Sometimes it is easy to forget that. But I want to take this opportunity to remind myself, and maybe some of you, of that truth.

Even those people who might have brought us pain. They made us stronger, tougher, and helped us to be more confident. As long as we don't, and never, give up on ourselves.

And those who have helped us, all those beautiful souls and remarkable companions of ours, they continue to make this journey so much more treasurable and incredible. We need to remind ourselves to let them know that we appreciate them.

The part of the journey that was covered in this book also taught me the importance of having a solid financial foundation and security, without which many challenges in life become much more unbearable. With the savings habit that I had built since my first weeks in New York City (minus the bologna-ketchup-sandwiches and the Big Mac's), and with the help and knowledge from so many great resources, I have been blessed to build and

ACKNOWLEDGMENTS

enjoy solid financial security and an extraordinary life. And I have devoted most of my time and efforts of the recent years in helping others on their quests to achieve such financial security as well.

What I have also learned is that some seemingly small gestures – a helping hand, a few minutes' time, an encouraging word, or even a meaningful look – can mean a world of a difference to a person in need. Many of my friends don't even remember how they had helped me, or realize what their help meant to me. But I am forever grateful for what they had done or said when I needed it the most. And it has been, and will always be, my goal to give back, pave forward, and to assist those who I can help, in whichever way it may be appropriate.

So to all of you who were there for me, especially during that special year of my life that was covered in this book: Chengyun, Faye, Connor, Wendy, John, Martin, Shirley, Ray, Quinn, Francesco, Matt, Steve, Jason, Stacy, Jonathan, Chris, Cindy, Daisy, Nancy, Violet, Howard, my college friends, professors at NYU, and so many more, *THANK YOU!* And I want to thank those of you who took the time and interest to read (parts of) the draft versions of this book. Thank you for your valuable feedback and permissions to publish this book.

Big thanks to those, who, even though didn't know me back then, took the time to read my manuscript in various shapes and forms, and provide your valuable feedback: Lori, Gwen, Dr. Forman, Teri, Niko, Robbie and Melody. Your feedback and encouragements have helped me tremendously in editing my manuscript, and coming up with the courage and determination to release this work.

I also want to thank the educators and students at Palomar Community College involved in its Bravura project. Attending the Bravura Gala in 2018 inspired me to put the goal – "Write a book" – down for 2019. And now you have it. I appreciate Professors Versaci and Smith from the English Department at the College for taking the time to email their advice and recommendations for me to learn more about memoir writing.

To Maria, who is amazingly talented in so many things, including biotech, finance, and photography. Thank you for the fun afternoon when you took those great pictures of me, where my portrait on the back cover of this book came from.

To Lori, what an incredible friend you are! You are one of the smartest, most beautiful and successful people I know. Thank you for taking your highly valuable time to not only read my manuscript (twice!), but painstakingly editing it. Thank you for all the wonderful feedback you've given me. I also want to thank you for everything you've done for me, for all these wonderful years that I have had the privilege to know and befriend you. If I ever write another memoir, you and your white Miata will be in it. That is a promise.

To my loving family: my parents, *Gege*, my husband, my kids, my in-laws, thank you. Without you, your love and support, I would not be who I am today. Nor would I have the courage to write and publish this book.

I also want to thank you, my dear reader, for taking your time to read this book. I hope you enjoyed this journey while traveling with the 22 - 23 year-old me. I hope you have shared a few laughs and maybe shed a few tears. And if you could be so inspired to write down a couple of lines, a few pages, or several books of your own thoughts and stories. Then I will be happier still. I truly believe that sharing life's experience can help us all to be better connected, and gain more understanding of ourselves and each other. It could make this wonderful world an even better place, and make this beautiful country an even stronger nation.

Please feel free to share your thoughts and stories with me if you'd like. I'll be honored and delighted to receive and read them.

Forever yours,

Li
San Diego, California, USA.
Westbound.Book@gmail.com
InstaGram: @westbound.book
Facebook: @westboundbook

Made in the USA
San Bernardino, CA
25 June 2019